ART DECO
THE EUROPEAN STYLE

ART DECO
THE EUROPEAN STYLE

SARAH MORGAN

ARLINGTON
PRESS

This edition published 1990 by
Arlington Press
130 Arlington Road
London NW1 7HP

Produced by Bison Books Ltd
Kimbolton House
117A Fulham Road
London SW3 6RL

ISBN 1-871378-73-7

Printed in Hong Kong

Page 1: This clock by Van Cleef
and Arpels, 1926, is designed in
the form of a Japanese temple
portico; the signs of the zodiac
replace numerals.

Page 2: *The Flame Dancer* by
Ferdinand Preiss, cold-painted
bronze and ivory, c. 1930, is
typical of his later, more
contemporary style and
illustrates the high quality of his
ivory carving.

CONTENTS

INTRODUCTION

Opposite: Gerrit Rietveld's Red-Blue chair, c. 1917, reflects the emphasis laid on straight lines and primary colors by the Dutch De Stijl movement, which adopted an intellectual approach to design and rejected ornamentation.

Art Deco is not a clearly defined movement; the term covers a period in the history of the decorative arts (including a portion of the fine arts), a style which developed from just prior to World War I and which lasted on into the 1930s, though not in quite the same form.

Art Deco began as a specifically French or even Parisian creation and remained essentially a French style. Yet many designers elsewhere in Europe were influenced by French design and worked in the same, or a similar, idiom. Whether or not a piece displays French influence does not always define its claim to be called a work of Art Deco. Important variants of Art Deco were created in countries other than France, while some designers based their designs less obviously on the French style but still produced work that captured that same spirit. With hindsight a remarkable similarity of theme and style can be detected in work produced throughout Europe and America in the interwar period.

Some of the French designers of Art Deco labeled their work '*style moderne*', but no really comprehensive general term existed to cover the various manifestations of the style until the 1960s. The phrase is derived from the title of the Exposition des Arts Decoratifs et Industriels, which was held in Paris in 1925 and was an important landmark in the history of Art Deco.

The early years of the twentieth century, known as the Edwardian era in England and the *belle époque* in France, represent rather the last moments of an extended nineteenth century than the beginnings of a new one, despite the promise of ever-increasing technological advancement. For the turn of the century launched Europe into a second Industrial Revolution. Cars began to fill the streets, buses and taxis were becoming motorized, and the railway and underground networks were expanding. Electricity and central heating were gradually entering homes, as were the telephone, the wireless and the gramophone. The capitalist economy was booming, and until World War I only a handful of socialists spoke of its imminent collapse. The bourgeoisie hardly felt the threat of socialism; pre-war Europe was in a very confident state of mind.

Yet society was on the brink of radical change, and the symptoms of that change were becoming increasingly evident. The new and more efficient modes of transport, the advances in communication, the growth of the media and the changes taking place in the home were all harbingers of the new age, signaling the beginnings of a social upheaval that would lead among other things to the emancipation of women and improved conditions for the lower classes. As if fearful of the future, however, the wealthy upper classes studiously ignored the changes that were taking place, and resolved instead to prolong the past with a kind of mad intent, holding fast to the rigid class structure as if to a sinking ship.

As far as the arts are concerned, they were far ahead in predicting (and instrumenting) change. The turn of the century marks the point at which the Modern movement in the fine arts and literature was born. It is important to remember that this revolution took place not during the war or immediately after, but some years before. In 1905 the Fauves burst on the

Right: Süe et Mare's *Parfums d'Orsay* shopfront, c. 1925; Parisian high style Deco was in many ways epitomized by the work of Süe et Mare.

scene with their brilliant color effects and their exaggeration of form and perspective. It was the beginning of the break with naturalism and the move towards abstraction.

The style that preceded Art Deco in the history of the decorative arts was Art Nouveau, which developed in the 1880s and reached maturity at the turn of the century. This was something of a compromise between advancement and the deliberate refusal to face the future that was characteristic of its epoch. It was modern in the sense that it sought to break with tradition, and the historical plagiarism that dominated the arts through the nineteenth century, and to establish a new decorative vocabulary that could be applied almost universally. On the other hand it was retrogressive in the sense that its exponents did little to make it available to anyone but the very wealthy or to adapt it to the machine, but instead raised the designer-craftsman to the status of artist and concentrated on the production of hand-crafted *pièces uniques* for an elite clientele. The Paris exhibition of 1900 marked the demise of Art Nouveau as a fashionable style, though it was popularized in a degraded form until well into the 1920s.

In retrospect, the graceful lines and delicate tones of Art Nouveau, although for a while considered quite avant-garde, seem to reflect the decadence of the old world and therefore seem doomed to die the same death. It is significant that Art Deco, though it owes much to Art Nouveau, scarcely reproduces those sinuous lines. By and large the change is abrupt; straight lines and geometrical forms take the place of those indulgent meandering curves, and in its mature style Art Deco's boldness, dynamism and compact forms are a complete antithesis to Art Nouveau.

Art Deco developed in response to the general pressure to adapt to the modern world and, specifically, was a stage in an already burgeoning revolution in the decorative arts. As the pace of change accelerated in the early twentieth century, it became clear that the lingering traces of the previous era needed to be eradicated and the environment to be redesigned. Three countries, France, Austria and Germany, came to the fore in the search for a suitably modern decorative idiom.

Art Nouveau had begun as a serious attempt to integrate art into social life and to establish a new style by looking to nature, but it quickly degenerated into a celebration of decoration for its own sake. In England the architect Charles Francis Annesley Voysey influenced a movement opposed to Art Nouveau and shortly afterwards in Vienna the architect Otto Wagner, inspired by the work of Charles Rennie Mackintosh, began to advocate the adoption of a new form of design that abolished curves and was based on geometrical forms.

Left: Wells Coates 'AD65' radio for Ecko, 1933. Designers of mass-produced objects such as fridges, radios, cameras and clocks took their inspiration from Deco.

Charles Rennie Mackintosh adapted Art Nouveau in an individualistic fashion and tamed the flamboyant curves, introducing them into a geometrical play of verticals, horizontals and spatial volumes. His work used ornament to set off a more severe, sober and functional style and was an important precursor of Art Deco.

Below: Cover design by Aubrey Beardsley for *The Yellow Book*. Beardsley's sinuous graphic style and decadent manner was as great an influence on Deco designers as on the masters of Art Nouveau before them.

The Yellow Book
An Illustrated Quarterly
Volume III October 1894

Price $1.50 Net

London: John Lane
Boston: Copeland & Day

Price 5/- Net

Right: Josef Hoffmann's footed silver dish with cover, 1902. Hoffmann was more severe and rigorous in his tastes than other members of the Vienna Secession, employing a strict geometry in his designs for furniture and metalwork.

Far right: Charles Rennie Mackintosh's armchair with colored glass insets, 1904, is an example of his tamed and geometrical Art Nouveau style.

As a result of Wagner's teaching a group of artists was formed in Vienna who broke away from the Academy and set themselves up as the Vienna Secession. Their common resolve was to abolish Art Nouveau and replace it with something more rigorous and modern, and they were greatly influenced by the work of Mackintosh and the English Arts and Crafts movement with its focus on craft production (a reaction to the shoddy industrialized goods produced in the nineteenth century). The lead-

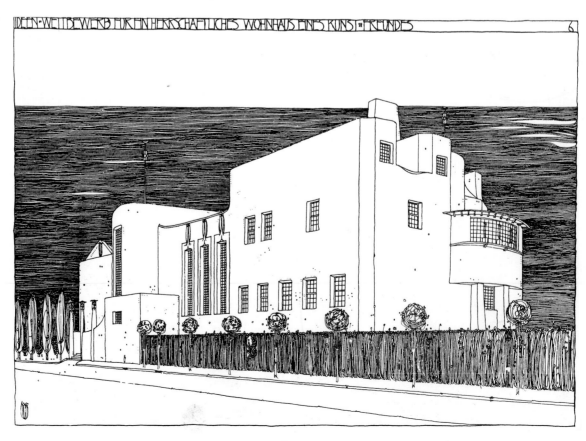

Right: Charles Rennie Mackintosh's sketch for a 'House for a Lover of the Arts', 1901. Notice the similarity to the Palais Stoclet (right), particularly in the block forms and the decorative grouping of windows.

ing members of the Secession were the architect-cum-designers Josef Hoffmann and Josef Maria Olbrich and the designer Koloman Moser. The general focus was on craftsmanship and industrial techniques were applied only rarely; this was essentially an expensive style that depended on rich patrons. Olbrich built the Secession headquarters in 1897-98; its blocked forms and stylized decoration, applied not indiscriminately but in an ordered and restrained manner, make it an important forerunner of Art Deco.

In 1903 the Wiener Werkstätte was established, under the joint direction of Hoffmann and Moser, to manufacture and sell the designs of the Secession artists. Their first important commission was the magnificent Palais Stoclet in Brussels, built for a Belgian coal magnate, which was begun in 1905 but not finished until 1911. Hoffman designed the building and numerous Werkstätte artists collaborated on its decoration. From the cutlery to the mosaic murals in the dining room, which were designed by Gustav Klimt, an astonishing homogeneity was achieved, an aspect of Austrian design that particularly impressed French and German designers. Another feature of the design throughout the building was the use of luxurious materials and the combination of floral and geometrical motifs and patterns. These elements too were absorbed into Art Deco, although rendered more lightly and gracefully by French designers.

Meanwhile, still in Austria, there existed a more radical movement headed by the architect Adolf Loos, a movement that for aesthetic

Above: Josef Maria Olbrich's Vienna Secession building, 1897-8, an important forerunner of Art Deco.

Left: The Palais Stoclet in Brussels, 1905-11, designed by Josef Hoffmann, the first major Wiener Werkstätte commission.

and ideological reasons sought to abolish ornament altogether. His ideas had more in common with the emergent German style.

At the time when the Vienna Secession was becoming established, Germany had a more pressing reason for finding a suitable modern style that could be applied to everyday objects and furnishings; it sought a foothold in the increasingly competitive European market. Through the initiative and encouragement of the government and the efforts of Hermann Muthesius, who headed the project, an organization named the Deutsche Werkbund was founded in 1907 whose members were both artists and industrialists. Their goal was to promote the application of new design techniques in industry, and so to improve the standard of manufactured goods. The Werkbund became the first organization to recognize the potential of the machine and the importance of industrialization in the new century. Muthesius made a lengthy study of English design and decided that the new style, like the work of the Werkstätte, should be based on the sober and functional forms of the English Arts and Crafts movement and the work of Charles Rennie Mackintosh, yet without the focus on

Below: This set of glassware designed by Adolf Loos is an example of the extreme simplicity of Modernist design.

the manual production of goods. He stressed the importance of maintaining a simple and unified style that was identifiably German.

Peter Behrens was a founder member of the Werkbund and successfully applied its tenets in industrial design and packaging, notably in his work for the company AEG. Later, as director of the arts and crafts school in Düsseldorf, he set an important precedent in his reform and modernization of art education.

As a result of the success of the Werkbund, a style began to emerge in Germany in the first decade of the twentieth century that was simple, smart and distinctly modern. The French were rather taken aback, when the Deutsche Werkbund exhibited a few interiors at the 1910 Salon d'Automne, to discover that the Germans had developed a strong new decorative idiom while they had been casting about for styles to revive as Art Nouveau waned. They had to admit its success, and much of the change that then took place in the decorative arts in Paris can be attributed to the influence of German design at this exhibition. Although Art Deco appeared to reject Art Nouveau wholeheartedly, it in fact retained many of the characteristics of its predecessor. Its attempts to be modern were half-hearted and it remained very much an expensive, hand-crafted luxury. It was almost as if the purpose of both styles was to exclude the machine by requiring elaborate tasks that only a craftsman could perform; Art Nouveau with its intricate carving, Art Deco with its complicated veneers and its emphasis on exquisite cabinetry. As a result decoration remained a major feature of the new style and the decorative fantasy world of flowers, women and fauna, which was partly inherited from Art Nouveau and partly from traditional classical-inspired design, was adapted and stylized in keeping with the new idiom. It is significant that a number of designers who had worked in the Art Nouveau style became early exponents of Art Deco; René Lalique, Maurice Dufrène, Paul Follot and Léon-Albert Jallot among others. From the beginning Art Deco was characterized by its likeness to Art Nouveau. While it responded to the pioneering work of the Werkstätte and the Werkbund in its search for a modern idiom that could be applied to all areas of design and its rejection of the outmoded curves and excesses of Art Nouveau, its emphasis on the manual production of goods and distrust of the machine excluded it from the avant-garde movements that were forming in northern Europe. Art Deco always represented a more conservative alternative to the extreme changes in design and production proposed by more radical groups.

Designers in Paris began to cast about for ways of interpreting the new developments in Germany and Austria in a French manner. For

Left: Two celebrities of the Deco period: Paul Poiret and Josephine Baker at a party *chez* Poiret.

mediately enchanted by the vivid color, the decorative exuberance of the sets and the sensuous nature of the dancing. The preoccupation of the Ballets Russes with Persian and Oriental themes, so exquisitely and lavishly rendered in the sets and costumes of Léon Bakst, rapidly became absorbed into French design. The couturier Paul Poiret, arbiter of taste to the new epoque, was responsible for introducing these new elements into women's fashion. Under his influence ladies donned turbans sprouting extravagant plumes, and loose jewel-colored gowns in satins or heavy brocades that wrapped and draped.

Poiret was a flamboyant character and enormously influential in establishing the new decorative mood. He applied himself to the creation of a new style of furnishing and interior design. Inspired by the Werkbund exhibits at the Salon d'Automne of 1910 and aware that France needed to reassert herself quickly in the field of design, Poiret visited Germany and Austria where he met designers, scrutinized their work and absorbed their ideas. He was full of admiration for what he saw, but disagreed with the methods of training young artists and the way that pupils were

Below: Chinese vase of the Sung dynasty, twelfth to thirteenth century. The restrained elegance of Oriental design influenced all disciplines, but was particularly apparent in the field of ceramics. Compare this vase to those of Lenoble and Decoeur.

it was important that France should uphold its traditional reputation for innovation and excellence in the arts and design and, on a more practical level, that she should combat the influx of foreign manufactured goods. A Société des Artistes Décorateurs had been in existence since 1901 and was active in organizing regular exhibitions. In 1903 the Salon d'Automne was founded, where designers and decorators were encouraged to exhibit alongside fine artists. This was a period when painters, sculptors and architects were becoming increasingly involved with design and the decorative arts.

Although some designers looked to sources such as traditional French provincial furniture for inspiration, the mainstream continued to draw on the styles of the late eighteenth century. The neoclassical style adapted well to the increasing urge to simplify forms; Jacques-Emile Ruhlmann was among its chief exponents. From early on his work was an absolutely simple, pared-down interpretation of neoclassical forms, and the high standard of craftsmanship that he maintained was also inspired by eighteenth-century craftsmen.

Art Deco was largely based on this neoclassical revival but it was also a very promiscuous style, borrowing arbitrarily from a variety of sources, particularly Oriental and Middle Eastern art forms. The arrival of Diaghilev's Ballets Russes company in Paris in 1909 triggered a fascination with these foreign sources and struck a note that resounded through the ensuing years, one of sexual liberation, gaiety and creative vigor. The Parisian public was im-

forced to adhere to an established style. He resolved to help create a new French idiom that did not suppress individuality but was fresh and spontaneous. When he returned to Paris in 1911 he set up the Atelier Martine (which he named after one of his daughters). Young, working-class girls were encouraged to sketch and paint from nature instinctively and with minimal tuition. The best results were made up into repeating fabric designs and rugs and were used for furnishing and fashion. The Atelier also manufactured furniture and provided an interior design service. One of the aspects of German and Viennese design which had particularly appealed to Poiret and many other French designers was the harmony and coherence that was achieved in their interiors. French designers sought to emulate this homogeneity, hence the emphasis placed on the *ensemble* (the total design of an interior) and the *ensemblier* (its designer).

Martine furniture was clearly influenced by Werkstätte work, but was less severe in style. Interior schemes were equally inspired by the sumptuous exoticism of the Ballets Russes sets. The simplicity of the furniture was offset by gay colored fabrics, wallpapers and rugs, and heaps of bolsters and cushions in luxuriant

satiny fabrics. The style Poiret propagated was a charming blend of naïvety and sophistication. This combination was particularly evident in objects and furniture whose design was based on primitive or early art forms, but made sleek and urbane through stylization, intricate craftsmanship and the use of lavish materials. This became an important feature of Art Deco, as did the idea that the simple and sometimes severe furniture designs of Art Deco should be set in a richly patterned context. Even when furniture was pared down to the simplest tubular steel and plain upholstery, a brightly colored carpet or patterned wallpaper enlivened the setting.

The craze for things exotic and eastern begun by the Ballets Russes came at a time when designers were avid for new ideas and motifs from outside the sphere of French historical styles. New influences were quickly absorbed into the Art Deco vernacular. The restraint and elegance of Oriental design and the high standard of craftsmanship were much admired, and inspired the light mannered quality and elegance of Art Deco. The Oriental art of lacquerwork was incorporated into the Art Deco repertoire early on by artists such as Jean Dunand and Eileen Gray. Its smart glossy finish and its versatility – it could be absolutely plain or highly decorative – made lacquer one of the single most popular materials of this period, and it was applied almost universally; to screens and sofas, vases and jewelry, and even to fabrics.

The arts of ancient and primitive civilizations provided Deco with a rich source of motifs and decorative themes. An enthusiasm for African art filtered through from Cubism, and coincided with the fascination with Negro culture that spread across Europe following the arrival of the black jazz musicians from America. The highlight of this influx was the sensational cabaret artiste Josephine Baker, who was propelled to stardom when she was barely twenty, wearing only a string of bananas. The colonial exhibitions that were held in Paris in 1922 and 1931 also helped to familiarize designers and public alike with African art.

In 1922 the tomb of Tutankhamun was discovered and there followed a frenzy of Egyptianizing. Jewelry, handbags, cigarette cases, furniture and even buildings were adorned with, often implausible, Egyptian-style motifs. The best designers studied the Egyptian treasures carefully, and were equally careful to extract whatever elements of Egyptian design were best adapted to their work. Also influential on design, and particularly on Art Deco architecture, were the Mayan and Aztec civilizations of Pre-Columbian America.

It was not uncommon for designers to create fantastical, hybrid styles that combined elements of many ancient and archaic art forms. It is important to recognize that by and large Art Deco designers did not copy slavishly from these sources. There were no scholarly 'quotes'. What these art forms offered was an invaluable source of abstract, geometrical or figurative imagery. As Art Deco designers began to respond to the changes taking place in the arts, and the pressure to 'modernize' grew stronger, the influence of this source material

provided a means by which Art Deco could modernize itself without sacrificing its decorative element.

Of all the avant-garde art movements that came into being in the early twentieth century – and most exercised an influence of some sort on Art Deco design – Cubism was the most important for the early development of Art Deco. 1907, the year when Picasso finished painting *Les Demoiselles d'Avignon*, marks the birth of Cubism; Picasso drew widely on influences such as archaic and African sculpture and Egyptian art, as he sought to break with tradition and devise a new means of expression in painting. *Les Demoiselles* heralds an important move away from realism and toward abstraction.

Picasso and Braque developed Cubism from its infancy, creating an art which sought to examine three-dimensional form and the nature of representation. Forms were fragmented, simplified and abstracted, and traditional perspective was abandoned in favor of a multiple-viewpoint perspective. The influence

Above: Russian peasant costume designed by Natalia Goncharova for the Ballets Russes production of *Le Coq d'Or*, 1914.

Left: Bed of the Divine Cow from the tomb of Tutankhamun, c. 1350 BC; stylized animal motifs borrowed from pieces such as this were incorporated into Deco design.

Above: A seventeenth-century Japanese Sutra lacquered storage box with lotus petal design. The decorative quality and sleek aspect of Oriental lacquerwork was greatly admired by Deco designers.

of Cubism quickly spread through the arts, and became absorbed into the decorative arts too – the emergent Art Deco. Art Deco designers adopted superficial aspects of Cubism, incorporating its angular, faceted quality into their stylistic vocabulary and using a 'Cubist' treatment of form to update motifs. This angularizing and faceting was a means of disciplining and homogenizing all the disparate elements of Art Deco. In its later phase, abstract designs of interlocking geometrical forms were applied as ornament and the Synthetic Cubist experiments with collage became incorporated into design in the tendency to juxtapose different materials.

• When Art Deco first came into being before World War I, an atmosphere of excitement and innovation was bubbling to the surface all over Europe and particularly in Paris, where new revolutions in the arts were constantly brewing. From America came jazz musicians, night clubs and tales of the towering constructions being erected in New York. When the war came it left everyone a little subdued, but nothing could really halt the march toward modernity. In many ways the urge to forget its horrors and losses drove society on at an even greater pace. Youth was adulated, and women were liberated. Style and lifestyle are intimately related and early Art Deco reflected the light-hearted, furious enjoyment of life. It was the Jazz Age, the Roaring Twenties, *Les Années Folles*, as it was variously styled; a time of cars, cabarets, cocktails and flappers.

The 1920s were a time of liberation in many senses, and were notoriously sexually permissive. The naked female image abounded as a decorative motif and as a theme for painting and sculpture, offering an opportunity to indulge in a little eroticism, but also a potent symbol of modernity. The flapper girl with short hair and bared limbs stood for the new age. It was in this period, too, that advertisers began to recognize the advantages of using the image of the liberated, provocative, modern young woman to attract potential buyers.

After the war a new class of patron began to come to the fore, ousting the old *fin-de-siècle* aristocracy which was rapidly declining in power and wealth. The post-war spending spree that these *nouveaux-riches* embarked upon gave a special impetus to the new style. The luxury products of Art Deco became the emblems or status symbols of this new aristocracy. Under their patronage Art Deco became a style that reflected the new wealth, an elitist style that only the very rich could afford.

The extravagant lifestyle of the rich was epitomized in the great ocean liners that journeyed back and forth between Europe and America. In this period they were larger and faster than ever before, combining the style and extravagance of the old world with the technology, speed and comfort of the new. Under French influence, they were increasingly conceived as showcases of national design. The first luxury French vessels were launched in the early 1920s, culminating in the magnificent *Normandie* which made her maiden voyage in 1935. A tenth of the total cost of the ship was reputedly spent on interior decoration; most of the major designers of the period collaborated on its decoration.

From its rather hesitant beginnings Art Deco soon became a coherent and easily recognizable style, embracing all branches of the decorative arts. This was partly due to the emphasis placed on collaboration and achieving a unity of design in an *ensemble*, and partly also to the interdisciplinary skills of its practitioners. In no other period had artists been so versatile, acquiring skills in a whole range of crafts and disciplines and thus helping to spread the new style.

The establishment of large companies offering Art Deco furnishings and interior design schemes did much to publicize and consolidate the style. Ruhlmann set up his company in 1919 and in the same year Louis Süe and André Mare founded their Compagnie des Arts Français, both aiming to provide a complete decorating service. The growing number of magazines concerned with design and decorating also helped to promote and spread the style.

An important homogenizing influence on Art Deco was the 1925 Paris Exposition. It was 18 years in the planning, and the idea of presenting a coherent front to the rest of Europe must constantly have been in the minds of its organizers and contributers. It was particularly important in the development of Art Deco abroad, influencing design throughout Europe and in America.

At the same time it is important not to overemphasize the unity and rigidity of the style. The Paris Exposition is generally agreed to

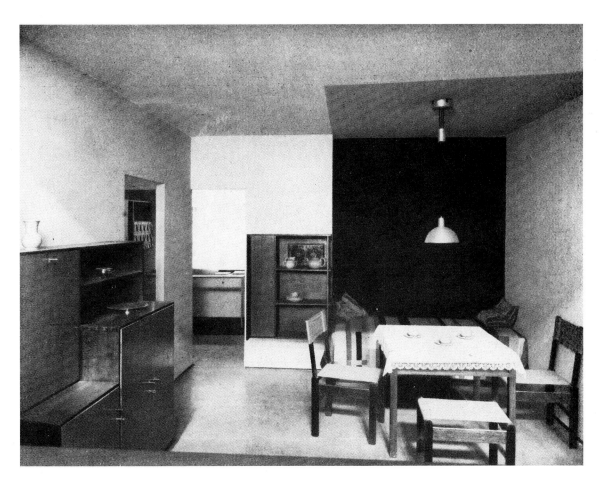

Below: *Camouflaged Ships in Dry Dock – Liverpool*, 1918, by Edward Wadsworth. He was a founder member of the British Vorticist group, which inspired a stark and dramatic decorative style.

mark the demise of the floral, elaborate and highly patterned style based on traditional French design which is best described as 'high style' Art Deco. This gave way to a mature phase dominated by the influence of Modernism, which can be labeled 'modernistic' Art Deco. The two phases are clearly closely related, however; Art Deco, though an evolving style, continued to be decorative, fashionable and eclectic and by and large it also retained its wealthy patrons.

The patronage of the great Parisian couturier Jacques Doucet helped to consolidate a middle style that bridged the gap between the decorative high style of Deco and its modernistic phase. In 1912 Doucet sold his fine collection of eighteenth-century furniture and art, in order to devote himself to the patronage of contemporary artists. By the mid-1920s he had replaced his old collection with a new one: paintings by Picasso, Braque, Matisse, Derain and the Douanier Rousseau among others, and sculpture by Brancusi and Zadkine. He had also assembled a considerable collection of African tribal art. These were housed in a new apartment at 46 Avenue du Bois. The apartment was furnished by a group of designers who worked in a remarkably coherent style and were undoubtedly influenced by Doucet's own tastes; their strong, simple and geometrical designs were inspired by Cubism as well as African and (to a lesser extent) Oriental art.

Deco's modernistic phase was also greatly influenced by the radical art movements such as De Stijl, Futurism, the Bauhaus and Constructivism. The Dutch De Stijl group was an active force in the interwar period. Its theories

were influenced both by Cubism and by Neo-platonist philosophy, and it aspired to utopian ideals concerning the unification of art and life. The members of De Stijl developed an entirely abstract or non-objective art that was based on the interplay of horizontals and verticals. Color was restricted to the three primaries, red, blue and yellow, and was used to accent the arrangement of planes in space. The architect Gerrit Rietveld applied their theories to the design of furniture and then to architecture. De Stijl work was stark, simple and functional, although functionalism remained secondary to the resolution of spatial problems.

The Bauhaus art school was set up by Walter Gropius in Weimar in 1919. The early years of its existence were devoted to Expressionism, but the arrival of the De Stijl artist Van Doesburg in 1921 helped to bring about considerable changes in its teaching and theories. He set about preaching the ideas of De Stijl to the Bauhaus and its pupils and, although there was some resistance at first, the influence was quickly absorbed. Marcel Breuer, who was then a pupil and later taught at the Bauhaus,

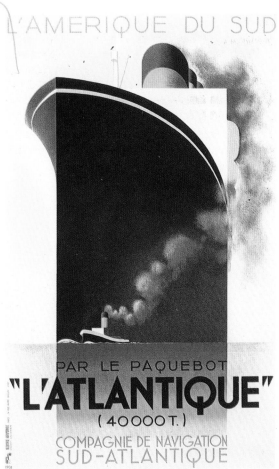

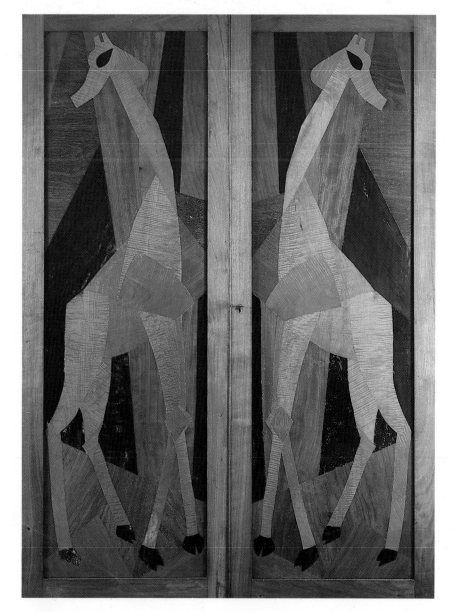

was particularly receptive to the influence of De Stijl. In 1922 the Russian Constructivist László Moholy-Nagy was appointed to the staff of the Bauhaus and introduced a further influence into the mix. He helped to eradicate the last traces of the Expressionist focus on craftsmanship and the notion of art as a spiritual revelation, and emphasized instead the relationship of art and industry, and the rational use of techniques and materials. The new Bauhaus style was geared for industry and bound up with revolutionary socialist theories, and was characterized by simple geometrical shapes, uniform areas of pure color and a complete absence of ornament. This Bauhaus style was particularly apparent from 1925, the year of the school's move to Dessau. The progressive atmosphere of the school nurtured great talents who helped to revolutionize the tools of everyday living and considerably influenced twentieth-century design. The Bauhaus is particularly famous for its pioneering of metal furniture design, which was to become one of the basic features of the modernistic Deco interior. It went on producing its innovative designs until the Nazis closed the school in 1933.

Intimately connected with developments at the Bauhaus was the Swiss architect Le Corbusier, who had worked for a time under Peter Behrens. His Esprit Nouveau pavilion designed for the 1925 Paris Exposition was clearly influenced by the Bauhaus and De Stijl. Le Corbusier deplored the prevailing obsession with ornament, and the starkness of his pavilion was in part a reaction against it.

The general aim of these pioneering Modernists was to promote change in the field of design and architecture by establishing exemplary models for furnishing, household objects and buildings which were functional and cheap to manufacture. Good design had to become available to people of all classes. They envisaged a time when the modern proletariat would inhabit high-rise blocks of white concrete and glass in apartments that were spacious, light and hygienic.

Left: Advertisement for the Delahaye motor car, c. 1930; note the streamlined design of the bodywork.

Below: Pablo Picasso: *Les Demoiselles d'Avignon*, 1907, a seminal Cubist work.

Right: The Coca-Cola bottling company plant in Los Angeles, 1936 (Robert V Derrah, architect), a good example of American streamlined Deco.

Toward the mid-1920s the rich decorative quality of the high style began to pall, and to give way to a more sober style. Designers began to respond to the Modernist developments, paring down forms and abolishing superfluous ornament. But their work was still invested with a Deco spirit; they continued to design for a rich elite, to use rare and luxurious materials, and in many respects they still held fast to the ideals of craftsmanship. Their use of abstract patterns and the build-up of forms shows a decorative quality that also distinguishes their work as Art Deco; it seems that designers assimilated the forms but not the doctrine of Modernism. The gloss of lacquer, shiny chrome and highly polished rare wood veneers maintained a chic and exclusive quality. Under the influence of the Bauhaus, craftsmen turned to re-examine the traditions of their craft and to seek decorative possibilities in the materials themselves. Applied ornament gave way to an abstract, decorative play of planes, forms and textured surfaces; floral motifs gave way to bold geometrical ones. In some cases the dividing line between Art Deco and Modernism is indistinct, and there are points at which the two styles converge.

In 1930 a group called the Union des Artistes Modernes was formed, with the intention of actively promoting a more sober style that made use of metal and other modern materials. The founding members came from various decorative disciplines and included Raymond Templier, Hélène Henri, Francis Jourdain, René Herbst and Robert Mallet-Stevens. As early as 1931 their campaigning had become redundant for their aims had by and large been achieved. The mood of frivolity had been sustained throughout the 1920s but was brutally destroyed by the Wall Street stock market crash of 1929 and the ensuing years of economic depression. The mad gaiety of the 1920s gave way to a period of social criticism and introspection, during which the modernistic tendencies of Art Deco were firmly established, decorative pomp and celebration of wealth were finally suppressed, and Bauhaus puritanism began to appeal more strongly.

Futurism inspired an obsession with modernity and the machine. Marinetti's Futurist manifesto, published in France in 1909, declared the need to demolish the past and celebrate in its place all the attributes of the modern world, above all speed and mechanical energy. The Futurists adapted the formal fragmentation of Cubism, seeking to express energy and movement in their work. Their vitality and preoccupation with speed became reflected in much Art Deco design, and Futurist methods of conveying vigor, movement and dynamism were adopted and exploited by Deco artists.

An important variant of modernistic Art Deco was the streamlined style. It is generally associated with American Art Deco, but was adapted to European design partly in response to the Futurist call to glorify speed and the machine. Streamlining exaggerated horizontal features and emphasized smooth curves, and was adopted in the design of cars, buses, trains and airplanes, in architecture, and to some extent in furniture design. It came to be applied to mass-produced objects such as fridges and radios to suggest modernity.

Most other countries of Europe made some attempt to update the decorative arts, inspired by the examples of Germany, Austria and France. Scandinavia was far ahead in developing a simple, cheap and functional style. Swedish glassware was particularly striking, echoing the mood of French Art Deco and evolving along similar lines. Germany developed a variant of the French style, although much heavier and less appealing, alongside the increasingly prevalent Bauhaus style. In Italy a modern style was evolved that was tempered with neoclassicism but showed some French influence, particularly in the area of graphic design. The Werkstätte style continued to dominate Austrian design through the 1920s, growing more floral and folky as it matured.

In England a group of artists known as the Omega group made an early attempt to modernize the decorative arts and, like the French, took their cue from avant-garde painting and particularly Cubism. The resulting style was in some ways comparable to early Deco, in that it was decorative and based on floral and animal designs as well as abstract patterns. In other ways, however, it was very different; furnishings were inexpensive with a deliberately hand-crafted feel. The Omega style had little immediate effect on British decorative arts; until the 1930s British design was still steeped in Arts and Crafts and reproduction styles. In the early 1930s Britain woke up to the developments that had been taking place in Europe, and French Deco began to exert a considerable influence. Vorticism, so named because of its intense focal perspective, was an English movement of the pre-war period which developed in response to both Cubism and Futurism; its influence contributed to the evolution of a strong decorative style in England. Like Futurism it was inspired by modern developments in technology, particularly in the fields of photography, engineering and architecture. The two editions of the movement's magazine *Blast* introduced important early innovations to graphic design and typography. Vorticism was also successfully adapted to the abstract patterning of decorative art design.

In Eastern European countries, notably Poland and Czechoslovakia, a style evolved which drew on the influence of Cubism and the decorative Wiener Werkstätte manner but was based on traditional folk styles. Czechoslovakia in particular developed a strongly Cubist style that has much in common with Art Deco.

From being a style created for an elite, Art Deco inevitably became popularized. It was apparent early on that Deco had tremendous selling power in terms of design, packaging and advertising. Many of its exponents were employed by manufacturers and retailers to give their products an extra boost. The profusion of magazines, posters, new shops and galleries meant that the style became familiar to the man on the street and began to filter down to a mass market.

After the Wall Street crash, Art Deco lost many of its important patrons, and manufacturers were forced to look to a less moneyed clientele for their source of revenue. The pared-down forms of modernistic Art Deco were well suited to mass production, being inspired by the industrial Modernist style. Public taste proved to be better disposed toward Art Deco than the austere Modernist style, and the 1930s saw a wealth of cheap goods in materials such as bakelite and chrome which were copies or adaptations of expensive Deco designs.

Left: Bathroom designed for a Cecil B De Mille film of the early 1930s. Hollywood adopted and propagated a more glamorous streamlined version of the modernistic European style.

TOURISME

RENSEIGNE
MENTS DE
TOURISME·
AVIATION·
BILLETS·
DE CH·DE
FER NAVI
GATION·

Rob Mallet-Stevens
1925

1
THE 1925
PARIS EXPOSITION

The idea of holding an international exhibition of the decorative arts was conceived as early as 1907. Eighteen years went by before the exhibition was held – World War I intervened and partly as a result plans were endlessly delayed and rescheduled. The Exposition Internationale des Arts Décoratifs et Industriels Modernes eventually took place in Paris from April to October 1925.

It so happened that the exhibition fixed and focused on an important moment in the development of the decorative arts, and particularly in the evolution of Art Deco, when the high style was on the verge of giving way to the mature and designer's were allowing Modernism to lead them forward. Because of the hostility still felt so keenly after the war, Germany was not invited to participate and the exhibition was deprived of what would have been an important element – a Bauhaus exhibit. Nonetheless Modernism was a strong presence at the exhibition; the Russian and Czechoslovakian avant-garde and minority factions in other countries, including Le Corbusier and his followers, all made uncompromising and controversial statements about design.

The Exposition was an opportunity to publicize, both abroad and at home, the French Art Deco style in its confident maturity. Although designers had exhibited at the Salons over the years, this was their first opportunity to present themselves as exponents of a comprehensive style, embracing all branches of the decorative arts. In general terms it was a point of consolidation but it was also a point of departure, in that it marked the demise of the high Deco style and the spread of French influence through Europe and America.

The exhibition was intended to be entirely modern in character. The regulations of entry were quite insistent on this point and an Admissions Committee was set up to vet entries. America was frightened off by so exacting a requirement and, feeling it had nothing modern to offer, declined to take part.

The text of the 12-volume catalogue of the exhibition asserts definite Modernist sympathies. It advocates machine-age aesthetics praising purity of form, sobriety of decor, the exploitation of new materials. It discusses the state of the decorative arts at the turn of the century and the successful application of a modern style in most areas of the decorative arts. Yet it reflects an attitude that is not completely in tune with the ideals of Modernism. While the production of well designed inexpensive goods is encouraged, it is also made clear that the best design should be reserved for luxury goods.

It would be wrong, however, to assume that the Exposition was all about high fashion furnishings for the very rich. There were all kinds

Below: The Porte d'Honneur, designed by Henri Favier and André Ventre with metalwork by Edgar Brandt, showing the view through the exhibition grounds to the Invalides on the far side of the river.

Left: Detail of the Porte d'Honneur showing metalwork by Edgar Brandt.

spired swagged roofing, walls set with floral relief panels and a shopping mall beneath. Designers who could not afford to exhibit in their own pavilions had shops here.

The French put on a fine show; it must have seemed as though no expense had been spared on the part of the hosts. Everywhere there was some extravagant gesture or gorgeous edifice to dazzle the casual visitor. Fairgrounds were set up, gardens laid out, there were ballets, plays, concerts, fashion shows, fireworks and a thousand other entertainments which were intended to maintain an atmosphere of festivity and lavish hospitality.

At night the spectacular illuminations were a further source of wonderment; in the field of electric lighting nothing so imaginative and on such a grand scale had ever been seen before. Numerous fountains, those *leit-motifs* of Art Deco, were erected and spotlit to enhance the dramatic thrust of the water. Particularly effective was the Lalique fountain in glass; the translucent stem was lit from within and threw a diffused light onto the fine jets of water

of pavilions and constructions, some representing the humbler aspects of modern life, from village houses to hostels, schools and churches. Here the exuberance of high Deco was inappropriate, but some of these buildings and interiors successfully incorporated a mild adaptation of the style.

The exhibition was held in the centre of Paris; across the Alexandre III Bridge, along both banks of the River Seine, and stretching up to embrace the Grand Palais. Exhibitors were allotted a site with space to build a pavilion and garden. Since the pavilions were entirely temporary and everything was to be pulled down at the finish, they were built in the cheapest materials; wooden frames and plaster, or concrete.

Thirteen gateways were set up at intervals around the exhibition grounds. These were extraordinary erections, grandiose and fantastic in conception, many of them archetypally high Art Deco in style, with their exaggerated proportions and stereotyped decorative features. The main entrance, the Porte d'Honneur, was designed by Henri Favier and André Ventre and consisted of groups of columns, each one crowned by a stylized pyramidal fountain, stepped back from the main road. The fountain motif was repeated in Edgar Brandt's highly decorative openwork grille which linked each group of columns to the next. With the Grand Palais looming to the left behind the gates and the unbroken vista through to the far end of the exhibition ground, it was a dramatic entrance.

In order to disguise the *fin de siècle* exuberance of the Alexandre III Bridge, Maurice Dufrène designed an awning with Oriental-in-

Below: Renè Lalique's illuminated crystal fountain designed for the Paris Exposition.

Right: LH Boileau's Pomone pavilion of Au Marché, showing its massive stepped forms and abundant low-relief decoration.

surrounding it like a mist. At night the Porte de la Concorde by Pierre Patout was transformed into a series of glowing discs hovering above the trees, an effect achieved by lighting only the tops of the columns. The most ostentatious display was the publicity stunt put on by the Citroën company. Colored bulbs were attached to the four sides and up the height of the Eiffel Tower which, when lit, described a series of changing patterns and the company's name and logo.

Paul Poiret, who had been so much a catalyst in the development of Art Deco and had nurtured it in its infancy, was overtaken and left behind by the now nearly mature Deco style. He exhibited three barges which he moored by the Alexandre III Bridge and named *Amours, Délices* and *Orgues.* He had them gutted and redecorated by the Atelier Martine, still in the Wiener Werkstätte-based style he had introduced at least a decade before. *Orgues* was laid out as a night club, with chairs and tables arranged around a dance floor. The expense of this extravagant gesture, and the lack of enthusiasm generated by these rather charming but by now old-fashioned interiors, marked the beginning of Poiret's plummet into financial ruin. He was to die penniless in a charity hospital after many years of obscurity.

Nothing better exemplified the high Art Deco style than the pavilions of the four great department stores, all jostling for attention along the approach to the Invalides. They are in fact better described as caricatures of that style, so

fantastic, stagey and over-embellished were they. The opportunity to create exciting, temporary structures was a great incentive to designers to be imaginative and explore the medium. In this case, however, imagination ran to megalomania. The Maîtrise pavilion of Galeries Lafayettes and the Pomone pavilion of Au Bon Marché were massive forms, stepped and faceted to emphasize bulk and height with (particularly in the case of the Pomone pavilion) every available surface decorated in low relief. The façades of both pavilions were dominated by gigantic leaded glass panels in geometrical designs. The Primavera pavilion of the Grands Magasins du Printemps was the most absurd. Like an enormous primitive dwelling-place, it was crowned by a funnel-shaped dome set with glass pebbles. Two pillars flanked a gaping entrance of plain glass. Instead of the usual embellishments of statuettes and relief panels, plants sprouted from the tops of the pillars and around the base of the dome like a frill. The exhibits in these pavilions were an important element in the presentation of Art Deco at the Exposition. They represented the less expensive interpretations of the style and were extremely popular with the public.

Emile-Jacques Ruhlmann, René Lalique and Edgar Brandt made up the great triumvirate that dominated the Exposition, all exhibited widely, all of them were ecstatically praised by public and critics alike and all of them, in their different ways, were leading exponents of high Parisian Deco. Lalique had his own pavilion,

Left: The Primavera pavilion of Printemps, designed by Henri Sauvage and Wybo; the most fantastic and caricatured of the four department store pavilions.

Below: Detail of the Sèvres pavilion designed by the architects Pierre Patout and André Ventre.

decorated with low-relief glass panels, in which he exhibited both large-edition objects and *pièces uniques*; anything and everything that could possibly be cast or blown in glass, from jewelry and scent bottles to floor and wall panels – everything but furniture, which he had not then added to his repertoire. He also designed a dining-room in glass for the Sèvres pavilion, complete with illuminated coffered glass ceiling. Ruhlmann exhibited his work alongside objects by other major Deco designers in his own pavilion, the Hôtel du Collectionneur (home of a patron of the arts), built by Pierre Patout. The simplicity and elegance of his designs, the careful harmonizing of interiors and the sheer luxury of materials caused a sensation. His pavilion was a Pomone type stripped of its decorations and fuss. The forms were more or less the same, but Ruhlmann's building, except for a central relief panel, dared to flaunt its bare concrete. Interest had shifted to the build up of planes, emphasized by subtle horizontal delineation.

Other Art Deco designers prominent at the exhibition were Louis Süe and André Mare, representing high Art Deco at its best – floral but not fussily so, grand, opulent and emphatically based on traditional French styles. They designed and decorated a Museum of Contemporary Art in which they exhibited furnishings designed by members of their company, La Compagnie des Arts Français.

Of the specialist French companies exhibiting decorative wares there were three, all of

Above: Konstantin Melnikov's USSR pavilion was designed in the Russian Constructivist style.

signers drew others around them to work on every aspect of the interiors. It was an archetypal example of the spread and success of the style.

It would have been apparent to anyone assessing the state of French design at the exhibition that the Deco style was in the process of evolving away from its early expression, and that other foreign but related styles were at various stages of a similar evolution. Floral and geometrical motifs were equally abundant. Extravagant highly decorative palaces stood next to simple white concrete buildings, all in their different ways clamoring for attention. Bare concrete, metal and glass were the materials that best expressed absolute modernity. Mallet-Stevens had the Martel brothers design cubist trees in concrete for a garden he created on the Esplanade des Invalides – a gesture both humorous and emphatic.

A building like Mallet-Stevens' Pavillon du Tourisme was still very much an Art Deco building, despite the obvious influence of Modernism, but at first sight was utterly different in appearance from high style Deco. The slatted effect repeated over the entrance and on the tower is essentially a decorative play of planes, though it derives from Modernism and De Stijl – the stress on horizontal planes was to become an important feature of the evolved Art Deco style. This building was no less attention-seeking in its way than the department store pavilions. Proportions were exaggerated for effect, the decorative slate emphasizing the height of the tower and the low horizontality of the main building.

Many of the foreign exhibits displayed a modernity that was based on traditional types and some were barely modern at all. The Italian pavilion was a Deco revival of a classical building, though much more revival than Deco. The Japanese pavilion was traditional and picturesque in style but, rather inconsistently, it was highly praised in the official catalogue, the French being too enamored of its Oriental neatness, clean lines and functionality to admit that it was not particularly inventive or modern. The English pavilion was an extraordinary hybrid of styles. Many countries, particularly those of Eastern Europe leaned heavily on their own folk traditions for inspiration.

The Wiener Werkstätte exhibit shows that the Werkstätte style had grown away from the severe geometry of its early designs and had become rather graceful and feminine. Recurrent motifs were floral and figurative. The Czechoslovakian display was chiefly composed of simple and bold glassware – Cubism was still a dominant influence, as it had been a decade earlier. This dynamic modernistic style must have impressed the French designers. The Constructivist ceramics, graphics and paintings in the Russian pavilion were particularly

them important and long established, that had successfully integrated the new style into their production, often hiring independent artists to design for them. These were the gold and silversmiths Charles Christofle and the Baccarat glassworks, sharing a pavilion, and the Sèvres company which specialized in porcelain and stoneware.

Perhaps the single most concentratedly Art Deco collaborative effort was the French Embassy prototype, a project realized by the Société des Artistes Décorateurs, and partly funded by the state. Here, the evolving style was quite apparent, alongside the less avant-garde designs of artists like Ruhlmann, André Groult or Jules Leleu. Robert Mallet-Stevens designed the entrance-hall, Francis Jourdain the smoking-room and gymnasium, Pierre Chareau the study-library. In other rooms the collaboration was more intense; the main de-

admired, as was the Swedish Orrefors glass.

For foreign exhibitors and visiting designers, the Expo was a powerful influence and stimulus. The impact it had on the work of the English ceramicist Susie Cooper, for example, was obvious and immediate. She devised a highly individual and successful style, based on and as a result of having visited the exhibition.

Despite the absence of either a Bauhaus or a De Stijl exhibit (the Dutch government refused to allow De Stijl to participate, despite Van Doesburg's pleas), Modernism was represented by Le Corbusier's controversial Esprit Nouveau pavilion and the Russian pavilion, and to a lesser extent by the Czech and Danish pavilions. Le Corbusier caused controversy with his pavilion even before it was built, and the Ministère des Beaux Arts ordered the erection of a high fence around the area for the opening of the exhibition. The pavilion was uncompromisingly stark and completely devoid of decoration, and Le Corbusier, being forbidden to cut down a tree on the site, had incorporated it extremely successfully into his design. All this drew a good deal of attention to his presence at the exhibition. Unfortunately the furnishings were less successful – he filled the interior with unmatched pieces of office furniture and cheap bentwood chairs, with a few Cubist paintings hung about the empty wall spaces.

The public might not have liked the Esprit Nouveau, but if they looked about them they would have seen plainly that the Art Deco style was following behind at a discreet distance. The exhibition marked the mid-way point in the evolution of Art Deco. It was also fundamental to the dissemination of the style both geographically, through Europe, and socially, down to a popular level. When Deco threw its doors open to the public it became popular taste.

2
FURNITURE

The story of the birth, growth and waning of Art Deco is best begun with a study of the furniture of the period, from the beginning of the century to the mid-1930s. At first glance it is difficult to see any connection between the earlier style, still firmly rooted in historicism, and the spare angular creations of the late 1920s. Yet a progression can be traced: a clear and unbroken evolution that owes its impetus to social and economic change, the example of the fine arts and architecture, and the increasing influence of Modernism. A will to simplify and be modern is the guiding principle but this is tempered with a desire to maintain comfort, chic and a sense of luxury, and a refusal to give way to anonymity and mass production.

For some years into the first decade of the century, fashionable furniture design contined to be dominated by the Art Nouveau masters, but the popularity of the style was rapidly dwindling. Art Nouveau had failed to provide a lasting modern decorative idiom, and patrons and designers began to scorn its excesses, in latter years so insensitively plagiarized for the mass market.

Although no specific style was to develop for some years, designers and craftsmen were guided by a desire to abolish the decorative hyperbole of Art Nouveau and to reassert the superiority of French design. A more rigorous style was sought, one that could keep pace with developments elsewhere in Europe (chiefly in Austria and Germany) but which was also identifiably French; maintaining, or rather re-asserting, the French characteristics of luxury,

refinement and high standards of craftsmanship. There was a reversion to simple, classical, elegant shapes; designers began to revive French styles of the late eighteenth and early nineteenth centuries. These borrowed styles were brought up to date with unusual combinations of materials and a stricter application of ornament. Focus shifted to the elegant forms of the furniture and decoration became confined mainly to flat surfaces, enhancing the lines and planes of a piece.

All manner of embellishments for those flat surfaces were devised, and in all kinds of exotic and rare materials. Rich veneers became fashionable, often applied to a cheaper and more robust structure. Warm woods were prefered, or woods with distinctive grain patterns such as amboyna, walnut, palmwood, zebrawood, Brazilian jacaranda and the dark striped macassar ebony. Ebony was a particular favorite, always highly buffed to a deep glossy finish. Many of the woods used were extremely rare, brought from southeast Asia or Africa. Sometimes tooled *repoussé* leather was applied as a surface embellishment, or fine leathers and animal skins such as morocco, vellum, snakeskin or tortoiseshell (sliced very fine to near transparency).

After a lapse of nearly 200 years shagreen was revived as a decorative material. This was the hard scaly skin of a breed of dogfish, which was bleached and sometimes tinted. It was applied in small sections and its patterned texture greatly appealed to Art Deco designers. A fine ivory inlay was used as a complement to

Below: Livingroom designed by André Groult and illustrated in Jean Badovici's *Intérieurs Français* of 1925.

Left: This commode in silvered wood with incised decoration and silk tasseled handles was designed by the Atelier Martine; neat and geometrical in form with opulent touches.

shagreen or dark wood veneers; drawer pulls were carved from ivory and furniture legs were tipped in ivory. Sometimes a number of materials, silver, mother-of-pearl or ivory, were combined in a marquetry design.

Oriental lacquer, made from the sap of a tree and applied to wood or a metal ground to create a hard, bright, smooth surface, was immensely popular in the 1920s. Lacquering is a laborious process but can be used to achieve a wide range of decorative effects. Pigments or minerals can be used to color the lacquer, gold and silver leaf can be embedded in it, and it can also be carved or encrusted with ivory, mother-of-pearl or hardstones.

Despite the emphasis placed on high quality cabinetry and craftsmanship, designers tended not to be craftsmen themselves. Very few of the top designers had more than a rudimentary technical knowledge. The large companies had their own cabinetmakers, while independent designers had their pieces made up by artisans working in the Saint-Antoine district of Paris.

Surviving records of private, commercial and government commissions show that Art Deco was a widespread taste, but the most significant source of patronage came from the fashion world. Led by Jacques Doucet and Paul Poiret, the top Parisian couturiers (most of whom were women – Jeanne Lanvin, Suzanne Talbot, Madeleine Vionnet) became the great promoters of the new style; they had their homes and their salerooms decorated with modish extravagance by their favorite designers and the results were much publicized. Initially the elaborate, high Deco style predominated, sponsored by wealthy patrons many of whom had recently joined the ranks of the rich and who sought a style that was both modern and comfortably within the bounds of tradition.

Paul Iribe is recognized by many as being the most important early exponent of Art Deco. He began his career as a caricaturist and his work was spotted by Poiret, who commissioned him to design an album of fashion plates. His talent was confirmed and Poiret set him designing furniture, fabrics, jewelry and rugs. In 1912 he was commissioned to decorate Doucet's apartment in the Avenue du Bois. Iribe's career as a furniture designer was short-lived, however, and by 1915 he had abandoned it for Hollywood and a new life creating film sets for Cecil B de Mille and others. Iribe's abilities as a

Right: Armchair by Paul Iribe, a major early exponent of Art Deco design whose work continued to show traces of Art Nouveau linearity.

Below: Armchair in macassar ebony, *repoussé* leather and ivory, c. 1925, designed by Clément Mère, another designer influenced by Art Nouveau.

draftsman are apparent in his calligraphic handling of design, which gives his work an insubstantial, brittle quality. He was one of the few Deco designers whose furniture continued to display the linear quality more associated with Art Nouveau – in his case a linearity that was always disciplined by an *ancien régime* elegance.

In the case of Clément Mère, it was his fondness for large areas of surface decoration that betrayed the lingering influence of Art Nouveau. As the Art Deco style matured, decoration became more controled in its application and Mère began to be criticized for over-embellishing his pieces. He started his career as a painter and worked his way from fine arts to applied arts, at first designing exquisite toiletry items and then graduating to furniture design in around 1910. This sort of career progression was typical of many Deco designers.

The basic structure of Mère's furniture was derived from eighteenth-century models but it was often almost completely covered in floral decoration, most characteristically in tooled *repoussé* leather. These floral designs were rather vague, loose and meandering, again reminiscent of Art Nouveau. There was also an element of Eastern exoticism in the richness of his textures, colors and decorative effects.

Another designer belonging to this early group was Clément Rousseau. He specialized in rich juxtapositions of fine materials, often in bold geometrical patterns, applied to simple structures that were based on late-eighteenth-century prototypes. His preference was for rich grained woods like palmwood or rosewood, which he set with stained shagreen (often in contrasting tints) or snakeskin. He was one of the first to revive the use of shagreen and to combine it with an inlay of fine bands of ivory.

Süe et Mare represent the fully fledged floral manner of high Art Deco. They were one of the first companies to offer a complete decorating service and helped to establish *ensemble* and *ensemblier* as keywords during this period. Spurred on by the example of the Deutsche Werkbund and Wiener Werkstätte, French furniture designers became increasingly concerned with the harmonizing of a room's décor. This did not mean a literal application of motifs from one piece to another, but rather a more imaginative general coherence of style, requiring a sense of proportion, pattern and color.

André Mare was a painter turned decorative artist. From around 1910 he was increasingly drawn to furniture and interior design, and in 1912 exhibited his 'Cubist House'. This was considered at the time to be terribly avant-garde but in retrospect was emphatically not; a little decorative angularizing on the facade was the only (very remote) reference to Cubism,

Above: This pair of chairs in rosewood, inlaid with sharkskin, ivory and mother-of-pearl, c. 1925, by Clément Rousseau, shows his juxtaposition of rich materials and simple classical shapes.

Left: Dressing-table and stool in burled ash and aluminium, 1933, by Süe et Mare, who found themselves obliged to keep pace with changes in design but were never really at home with the modernistic style.

and furnishings including fabrics, wallpapers and rugs; smaller items such as clocks and mirrors often also sported floral clusters.

There is nothing aggressively modern about Süe et Mare's work, and they said themselves that they did not aim to be avant-garde but simply to create pleasant and comfortable surroundings for their customers. Their interiors were indeed comfortable, colorful and warm, with densely patterned walls and floors. In 1921 they published what might be called a manifesto, *Architectures*, in which they justified their adherence to past styles. They represented those designers who reacted against Modernism and who stood resolutely for comfort and a sense of luxury and repose in an interior, which they said was needed more than ever before in the modern age, with all its stresses.

When Art Deco matured into its modernistic phase, Süe et Mare made a rather grudging attempt to adapt their style – in the march towards Modernism they brought up the rear. Despite their attempts to keep pace with fashion, they suffered financial difficulties in the late 1920s, and in 1928 their company was taken over. Nowadays Süe et Mare pieces are much sought after and fetch fantastic prices, rivaled only by works by Ruhlmann.

Also working in the traditionalist vein was Jules Leleu, whose simple forms, overlaid with a veneer of warm woods, were unremarkable and often derivative but for a characteristic scattering of tiny leaves and flowers inlaid in ivory and mother-of-pearl. This flowery signature made his work unusually fresh and charming. He was one of the few designers to execute his own designs, and his cabinetry was always of the highest quality.

André Groult began to exhibit at the Salons around 1910. His work was simple and his forms comfortable and solid; most of his pieces were designed to co-ordinate with the soft muted colors of paintings or wallpapers by Marie Laurencin. His most famous *ensemble* was the lady's bedroom in the French Embassy at the 1925 Exposition, with its curved forms clad in pale shagreen and its *bombé* chest of drawers in shagreen trimmed with ivory (the shagreen paneled to emphasize the swollen contours) – an extraordinary piece, with a faint, erotic suggestion of the female form.

Emile-Jacques Ruhlmann was in many ways the brightest star in the Art Deco firmament. His admiration for the *ébénistes* (cabinetmakers) of the late eighteenth century inspired him to strive for the highest standard of design and workmanship, and he can fairly be said to have attained those ideals in his work. He had an unfailing sense of elegance, proportion and harmony and a willingness to pare forms down to their minimum, displaying far greater restraint than any other designer working in the

which was never very apparent in the work of the traditionalists. The interior was in the pompous, bourgeois style that was to become characteristic of Mare's work with Süe. Louis Süe was trained as an architect, but he too became involved with interior decoration around 1910 and worked briefly for Paul Poiret. Süe and Mare met just before the outbreak of the war and began to work together when it was over. In 1919 they set up their Compagnie des Arts Français, more usually referred to as Süe et Mare, a partnership that lasted until 1928. They undertook architectural and decorative commissions and employed a prodigious team of collaborators who worked on schemes for embassies, shops, nightclubs and the luxury oceanliners. Companies likes theirs were forming in response to an increasingly competitive market and a general trend toward consolidating design services.

Süe et Mare's furniture was traditionally inspired, mostly by the Empire style but also partly based on provincial designs. A very superficially Cubist treatment is also evident. Carved tassels, *bombé* legs, formalized drape effects and curving contours are typical of their *oeuvre*: very much traditional forms gently brought up to date. They were also masters of the floral cluster, which was partly based on rococo motifs and partly derived from the conventionalized blossoms of Oriental art. Their company produced a complete range of objects

traditionalist manner. His furniture was highly exclusive, affordable only by a few.

Ruhlmann's first furniture designs were exhibited at the Salon d'Automne in 1913. He had no formal training in cabinetry, but made drawings which were scaled up and then passed on to a cabinetmaker. In 1919 Ruhlmann founded a company with Pierre Laurent. Slowly they built up their clientele and their workforce. His designs continued to be inspired by neoclassical furniture, and decoration was always minimal: just a hairline of ivory inlay sketching a pattern of diagonals, or a row of little ivory dots accenting form and line, a charming and brilliant device for softening the severity of his designs. In some cases silk tassels or ivory rings used as drawer pulls provided the only ornament. He employed Dunand to lacquer and Georges Bastard and Mme O' Kin Simmen to execute the ivory carvings and inlays he applied to his pieces. He used expensive warm woods such as amaranth, amboyna and ebony as veneers, while desks and dressing tables were inlaid with fine leathers such as morocco, snakeskin or vellum. In the late 1920s he developed a more minimalist and streamlined style making use of materials such as chromium-plated metal, silver and glass; his forms became squatter and more geometrical and lost their neoclassical references.

Left: Carved macassar ebony cabinet inlaid with silver and mother-of-pearl by Süe et Mare, 1927.

Below: Emile-Jacques Ruhlmann's *Grand Salon* from his Hôtel du Collectionneur at the 1925 Exposition; the painting over the fireplace is by Jean Dupas.

Ruhlmann was also a master *ensemblier*. He set his furniture in environments that were less hectically patterned and vibrantly colorful than those of most of his contemporaries, and achieved a sense of comfort and discreet opulence. He designed carpets, fabrics and wallpaper as well as tableware and lighting fixtures. His schemes were characteristically monumental, with lofty ceilings, gigantic cascading chandeliers and over-scaled wallpaper patterns. He drew around him the best of the Deco designers; the list of those who collaborated with him at the 1925 Exposition is impressive: Brandt, Decoeur, Décorchemont, Dunand, Jourdain, Legrain, Lenoble, Linossier and Puiforcat are the most notable. It was the Exposition that truly launched him and made his work known. His Hôtel du Collectioneur (home of a patron of the arts) was lauded by critics and public alike, and he became the focus of French pride in the reinstatement of its traditional supremacy in furniture design. Throughout his career Ruhlmann argued the importance of good craftsmanship and art for the elite. He was very far from being a Modernist, yet he contributed to the evolution of the Art Deco style by making pure, virtually undecorated forms fashionable.

Printemps was the first of the four great Parisian department stores to establish a design studio, Primavera, opened in 1912, and to market up-to-date furnishings by artists of repute at reasonable prices. The other stores followed suit in the early 1920s: Galeries Lafayettes with La Maîtrise, Le Louvre with Studium-Louvre and Au Bon Marché with Pomone. Recognizing that the growing and increasingly affluent middle class was becoming more discriminating, they replaced those manufacturers who had been foisting their outmoded designs on a dissatisfied public and met the demand for good design that was both relatively inexpensive and also fashionable and thoroughly modern in feeling. This was an important step on the road to making good design available to all classes through mass production.

Right: Cheval mirror in burled amboyna with fine ivory inlay, designed by Emile-Jacques Ruhlmann and showing his minimal use of decoration.

Below: Corner cabinet in lacquered rosewood inlaid with ivory and rare woods, 1916, by Emile-Jacques Ruhlmann.

The department stores offered a complete range of furniture and household goods, providing an interpretation of Art Deco that was neither extreme nor expensive. By popularizing the style they also helped to define it.

Maurice Dufrène was long associated with La Maîtrise studio, taking over its artistic direction in 1921. He was energetic and extremely versatile; he made an easy transition from Art Nouveau and later, with equal facility, adopted the modernistic style when it became fashionable. As long as the quality of goods was maintained, Dufrène was always in favor of using industrial methods of production to help cut costs. His style was unremarkable, a clever synthesis of the dominant trends in design.

The Pomone studio was run by Paul Follot from 1923. He was a staunch traditionalist and absolutely opposed to the mass production of art, but could not prevent Pomone from adopting the modernistic Deco style when he left. His taste for rather florid carving and elaborate surface decoration was no doubt carried over from his early association with Art Nouveau.

The high Art Deco style based on traditional forms did not have many important exponents abroad. In Britain there were a few half-hearted attempts to imitate the French style. At the Paris Exposition Sir Edward Maufe exhibited a desk in mahogany, camphor and ebony, gilded with white gold; its materials and tasseled

Left: Table in lacquered wood patterned with crushed eggshell, c. 1925, designed by Jean Dunand, a sculptor who turned first to metalwork then to lacquer.

draw pulls were inspired by French design, but it was altogether too heavy and inelegant to bear proper comparison. In general the British furniture industry was paralyzed by the lack of any creative opportunities and continued to turn out period reproductions of distinctly varied quality.

A few designers in Germany were working in the Parisian mode. They catered for a bourgeois elite, and based their designs on German

Below: Armand-Albert Rateau's bedroom for Jeanne Lanvin's home, 1920-22, one of his best known commissions.

Above: Jean Dunand's four-paneled screen in silver and black lacquer, c. 1928, shows his mastery of lacquerwork.

Below: Eileen Gray's furniture designed for Suzanne Talbot, c. 1920, is more abstract in style than her opulent early work.

Alongside the work of the traditionalists, which was fashionable up to the mid-1920s, there was a tendency among certain designers to explore the art forms of other cultures – notably of the Far East and the Middle East – in a move to break with past styles and create a truly modern idiom. The Cubists launched a fashion for tribal African art, which Doucet helped to absorb into the decorative arts and which stimulated in its turn a borrowing from other primitive and early art forms. Cubism itself was an important influence, encouraging designers to explore the decorative possibilities of geometric abstraction and the fragmentation of form.

These sources of inspiration had a very liberating effect on Art Deco, stimulating some highly original work which showed how far interpretations could diverge and yet still be part of the same style. In general the increasing urge toward simple forms and sparse decoration was more pronounced in the work of those artists exposed to non-French cultural influences, which reflected a more durable aspect of Deco, bridging the gap between the traditionalist and the modernistic styles.

baroque. Like the Parisian designers, they sought rich veneer and inlay effects but the results were undistinguished, lacking the grace of the French style.

Not every French designer who sought a new style around the second decade of the century looked back to French tradition for inspiration.

Paul Poiret set the example in borrowing from foreign themes and created a style that influenced both the traditionalists and those who sought a less 'historical' decorative idiom. He founded his Atelier Martine in 1911; by encouraging very young girls to draw and paint

Above: Eugène Printz's bedroom ensemble in palmwood, exhibited at the 1926 Salon of the Société des Artistes Décorateurs.

from nature, he established a source of spontaneous and colorful design. His style incorporated these designs and at the same time owed a great deal to the Ballet Russes and the flamboyant exoticism they had made popular. He launched a fashion for opulent interiors, with a rich confusion of pattern, color and texture on floors, walls and upholstery. Low divans and day beds were heaped with multicolored silk-tasseled cushions and pillows. Furniture was neat and geometrical, clearly influenced by Weiner Werkstätte design.

Armand-Albert Rateau was an unusual designer who developed a style based on Egyptian, Persian, Syrian and Antique art; walls, doors and screens were covered with delicate, stylized, silhouetted flora and fauna, with a few exquisite pieces of furniture in patinated bronze, oak and lacquer taking up the same motifs. He sculpted animals, charming, attenuated and graceful creatures which he arranged as supports to chairs, chaises longues, tables and standard lamps. From 1920 to 1922 he decorated Jeanne Lanvin's apartment on the rue Barbet-de-Jouy. The walls of the bedroom were hung with a blue silk fabric that was embroidered in white and gold thread in the Lanvin workshops. His famous low bronze table supported by four birds also stood in the bedroom. The bathroom was equally luxurious,

with an abstract pattern of marble inlay on the floor and a low relief stucco panel set into one wall depicting birds, deer and fronds. The fittings were in marble and bronze, and animal skins were strewn over the floor and furniture.

A sculptor who turned to metalwork and then to lacquer, Jean Dunand was one of the most versatile of the Deco designers. He learned the lacquer technique in 1909; tradition has it that he traded the secrets of his hammering technique for those of lacquerwork with the Japanese lacquer master Sougawara. He began by using lacquer to embellish his metal vases but became enamored of the technique and gave up metalwork to concentrate on the design of lacquered furniture, chiefly cabinets, panels and screens. The *laque arraché* method, which involved roughening and then gilding the top surface of the lacquer in order to achieve a gradation of tones, became a particular speciality of his. Dunand also revived the use of eggshell in lacquerwork and created a variety of different effects by sealing pieces of eggshell into a lacquer ground.

He established a system of collaboration with a number of designers, lacquering pieces for Printz, Ruhlmann, Legrain and others. He also executed decorative designs by Schmied, Jean Lambert-Rucki and Paul Jouve. Dunand's furniture was generally of the simplest design

with all the decorative interest confined to the lacquered surfaces. Early compositions tended to be strong abstract geometrical designs, while later on he began to diversify in response to the demands of a larger clientele, and added stylized animal subjects and *japonisant* or African figures to his repertoire.

Many of the most avant-garde and innovative designers of Art Deco were protégés of Jacques Doucet. He was an inspirational patron and influenced the development of a more modernist idiom. The designers he commissioned to decorate his home were encouraged to create interiors that would complement his collection of avant-garde art and Negro sculpture. The furniture was by Eileen Gray, Marcel Coard, Pierre Legrain and Rose Adler.

The work of Pierre Legrain was particularly marked by his long association with Doucet. He was discovered by Iribe and collaborated on the Doucet decorating commission of 1912 as Iribe's assistant. It was certainly due to his association with Doucet that he came to be interested in Cubism and African tribal art, which had a profound influence on his furniture design. This is evident in the fierce

geometry of his work; a prelude to the modernistic Art Deco style. A number of his pieces were directly derived from African tribal furniture. His work was simple and monumental, with a

focus on form and smooth surfaces, accented with color and minimal abstract ornament.

Eileen Gray was born in Ireland and settled in Paris in 1902. She trained as a lacquerer in

Above: Interior of Le Corbusier's Esprit Nouveau pavilion at the 1925 Exposition; the paintings are by Le Corbusier and Fernand Léger.

Opposite above: Le Corbusier, Jeanneret and Perriand's *ensemble* with three chairs in tubular steel, c. 1929; this type of innovative interior design was a significant influence on modernistic Art Deco.

Left: Bed in palisander, silvered metal, ivory and bakelite, c. 1930, designed by Marcel Coard in modernistic Deco style.

Opposite below: Pierre Legrain's black lacquered chaise longue incrusted with mother-of-pearl and upholstered with zebra skin, c. 1925, is typical of his simple geometrical style.

London and then in Paris under Sougawara. Her early furniture designs date from around 1910 and all the pieces were lacquered. This early work shows the influence of Oriental and African forms and motifs, yet is extraordinarily modernistic for the time. Colors are subdued and decoration minimal; all the novelty of design is concentrated on form and the enhancement of form. Doucet spotted her work at the Salon des Artistes Décorateurs of 1913 and the following year commissioned some furniture from her. The lacquered table she designed for him, with leg capitals carved in the shape of lotus blossoms, stems in ivory and dark-green lacquer, hung with huge silk tassels and rings of amber, is characteristic of her sophisticated and opulent early work. After the war she designed interiors for the milliner Suzanne Talbot (Madame Mathieu-Lévy), her first commission as an *ensemblier*. The rooms were dramatically bare but for the flying arabesque motifs that decorated carpets and walls and furniture was minimal. By this time she had abandoned figurative designs altogether in favor of abstraction.

In the mid-1920s she began to avoid the luxurious materials and the refinement and theatricality of her early style to concentrate on designing functional, compact, multi-purpose pieces intended to inhabit Modernist spaces.

At about the time that Marcel Breuer and Ludwig Mies van der Rohe were introducing tubular steel into their designs, she was doing the same. This change of direction corresponded to her growing fascination with modern architecture and Modernist theories. Her later work is truly Modernist in intent and cannot be considered as Art Deco.

After 1925, when the first experiments with tubular steel furniture were being made and the theories of the Modernists were becoming familiar and even appealing, Art Deco began to adapt to the new design currents. The new interiors were created partly in response to the change in building styles; apartments were smaller, lighter and more practical and required furnishings that were both compact and functional.

Many of the changes that came about in the decorative arts were due to the influence of the Bauhaus, which emphasized the use of new materials, the improvement of cheap manufacture and the creation of models appropriate for series production. The function of an object was the prime dictator of its design and so ornament became redundant. The Bauhaus artists were among the first to create tubular steel furniture, and much of this furniture, such as Marcel Breuer's cantilever chair, is so simple and archetypal that it has remained in production ever since. The influence of De Stijl, with its emphasis on the build-up of planes, also became absorbed into Modernism, particularly through the work of the architect and designer Gerrit Rietveld.

Le Corbusier played a fundamental role in the dissemination of Modernist theories, and helped to publicize and further the innovations of the Bauhaus. In collaboration with the designer Charlotte Perriand he created three chairs in tubular metal, all important prototypes in the history of design. Eileen Gray's Modernist work includes pieces that were multi-purpose and movable, made from tubular and perforated metal, glass and celluloid. She developed almost a mania for designing furniture that would pivot, swivel, fold away or slide to and fro on runners. Her Transat armchair is a famous piece, based on a deckchair design, with a padded seat slung on a lacquered and chromed frame.

The bentwood chairs that Thonet had patented in the nineteenth century were acknowledged as an important influence on these designers; Le Corbusier, for instance, filled his Esprit Nouveau pavilion at the 1925 exhibition with them. A number of designers recognized, virtually simultaneously, that simple lightweight structures in tubular steel similar to Thonet's bentwood frames would be easy to mass produce and could represent an attractive and versatile point of departure for a new design aesthetic. One of the great advantages of

metal was that it withstood the drying effect of central heating which was so damaging to woods. The rise of Modernism had much to do with the introduction of metal furniture. Initially many people put up a great resistance to metal, condemning it as too clinical and characterless. Le Corbusier's tubular chairs, particularly his chaise-longue, perplexed and enraged the public. The group of Art Deco designers who took up metal tubing and demonstrated how it could be made chic and luxurious by the addition of rich materials – lacquer, leathers, marble and smoked glass – did much towards making it acceptable. Inevitably machine-age simplicity and materials did become fashionable, and metal furniture gradually became standard in home and office.

Above: Pivoting nest of tables, c. 1924, by Pierre Chareau, who designed solid angular furniture to complement Modernist architecture.

Opposite above: René Herbst's diningroom, c. 1930, epitomizes the new stripped style.

Opposite below: Armchair, c. 1920, by Pierre Chareau.

The urge to pare down forms and abbreviate ornament that was always a tendency in Art Deco, became quite exaggerated under the influence of Modernism. Yet Art Deco retained most of its characteristics, its interest in elegance and refinement and its mannered quality. Furniture became simpler, more geometrical, compact and unadorned, with an emphasis on planes. The harmonized *ensemble* was still important but, in place of the cluttered effect of pattern on pattern, came a play of light and space and an arrangement of a few well chosen pieces.

From the early 1920s, a group of designers that included Francis Jourdain, Pierre Chareau, Robert Mallet-Stevens and René Herbst argued against the elaborate high style in favor of a stripped style that was absolutely modern and practical rather than primarily decorative. Some leaned more toward Modernist theories than others, but they all promoted an aesthetic that was modernistic; a stylish and distinctive version of Modernism. In their wake followed a group of less ardent modernistic designers, who compromised with strict Modernism and allowed the style to lapse back a little into a more comfortable and luxurious mode.

The Union des Artistes Modernes was established in 1930, its five founding members being Hélène Henri, René Herbst, Francis Jourdain, Robert Mallet-Stevens and Raymond Templier. Together they consolidated the attitude to design they had each pursued individually in their work, and at the 1930 Salon des Artistes Décorateurs they made a stand by exhibiting separately. Even by the next year their role had become redundant, since what they strove for had largely been achieved.

Although most Art Deco designers did not concern themselves with the problems of mass production and the democratization of design, the influence of Modernism, the new minimalism and the use of cheap, easy-to-manufacture metal furniture began to make modern design a general taste. Firms were established offering cheap furniture in metal or laminated wood; bright, simple and well-designed.

The architect Pierre Chareau designed furniture and interiors that complemented the new architecture; not furniture that rose on tapering legs, but solid, comfortable, sculptural forms, with an angularity derived from Cubism, which set off architectural features and enhanced the spatial setting. He had a fondness for contrasting curving lines with straight and overlapping pivoting planes, which allowed a table or desk to be enlarged or contracted and added subtlety and interest to the rigid geometry of Modernism. He also had a taste for unusual materials, although he did design furniture with traditional rich veneers and colorful patterned upholstery. He explored the use of glass and mirror; flat iron banding, which he used as a framework for some of his furniture; alabaster shades, for his lighting fixtures; studded rubber flooring, which he used throughout

Below: Pair of armchairs and small table covered in shagreen, c. 1927, designed by Jean-Michel Frank, who combined an austere line with expensive materials.

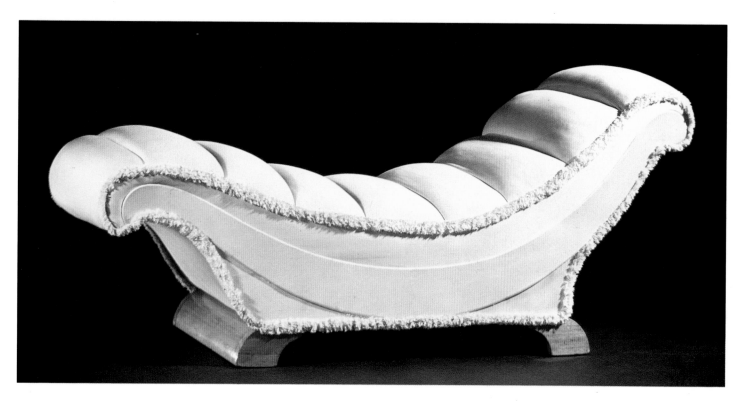

his Maison de Verre (constructed from 1928 to 1932); and he pioneered the use of plastic as a practical surface in children's rooms and bathrooms. The social implications and aims of the Modern Movement did not, however, concern Chareau. He worked throughout his career for a rich and discerning elite.

René Herbst designed uncompromisingly stark furniture from the start of his career in 1919, and denounced as outmoded the high Deco style. His best designs date from the mid-1920s when he was working a great deal in tubular steel. Shop fronts and window displays were his speciality. His designs were always very rigorous and logical, with a subtle elegance and careful balancing of proportions. Decorative details were few but distinctive and focused particularly on lighting fixtures; a

Above: Betty Joel's chaise longue in beechwood, upholstered in cream silk, c. 1930, bears comparison with the work of Frank.

Below: Sideboard and chair, c. 1930, by the Modernist architect Alvar Aalto.

lamp hovering like a butterfly over a dining table, or a standard lamp composed of a metal disk sitting at a jaunty angle atop a tubular metal support.

Robert Mallet-Stevens is more famous as an architect, but he did design furniture and interiors too and began exhibiting as a decorator around 1913. His furniture and interior design, like his buildings, are very angular and crisp, with a stress on horizontal planes that is almost decorative. Much of his furniture incorporates a slatted effect which is relieved or broken up by checkered or irregular geometrical patterning on carpets, curtains, upholstery, floor tiles and even light panels. This geometrical treatment was characteristic of the work of many modernistic Deco designers, and was related to the streamlining effect adopted from American Deco. Mallet-Stevens painted his tubular furniture in bright colors and used Hélène Henri's fabrics for upholstery.

As early as the first decade of the century

Francis Jourdain was preaching the need to unfurnish space and keep ornament to a minimum, letting the function of an object determine its design; his only concession to luxury was an occasional rich veneer. Later on he actively promoted the design and production of inexpensive furniture. His pieces were simple, geometrical and solid-looking, designed with the requirements of the smaller modern apartments in mind.

There were other designers who adopted the modernistic Deco style mid-career and promoted an expensive mannered version for a fashionable and rich clientele. Eugène Printz changed his style around the time of the Paris Exposition, having previously worked in an *ancien régime* idiom. An elegant interplay of curves and straight lines characterized his work, which was easy, refined and luxurious. Printz designed metal furniture as well as continuing to use expensive woods and developed a distinctive and innovative style.

Left: Denham MacLaren's table in glass, wood and chromium-plated metal, 1931, is typical of his idiosyncratic style.

Jean-Michel Frank designed in a very austere modernistic style but used expensive materials to create rich textured effects and a feeling of luxury. He covered walls and furniture in suede and parchment and upholstered in velvets, silks and suedes. His interiors were colored in natural tones and lighting was muted and concealed. He made straw marquetry his specialization, a laborious technique that required individual lengths of straw to be split and glued.

The new design current affected all designers, who were obliged to adapt in order to remain competitive. The result was that companies such as Süe et Mare made concessions to the new fashions and turned out superficially modernistic pieces that incorporated the new materials, especially metals and glass.

The high Deco style bypassed Britain, and by the late 1920s, when it was organized to compete with France and Germany, Modernism was the trend. Because this was not a style based on specific historical precedent, it was easily assimilated and British designers were soon contributing their own strong Modernist style.

Below: Betty Joel's kidney-shaped desk, c. 1930.

Serge Chermayeff introduced the first tubular metal furniture to Britain, which he marketed through the furniture store Waring and Gillow. He, Jack Pritchard and Wells Coates spent some time visiting the Bauhaus and absorbing ideas, and later set about applying the same approach to design in Britain. The company PEL (Practical Equipment Limited) was set up in 1931 and produced ultra-modern smart furniture along tubular lines. Tubular steel very quickly became popular and inspired all sorts of innovative designs. At the same time a good deal of cheap mass-produced furniture began to flood the market – insensitive renderings of modernistic themes, with indiscriminate use of geometric motifs and lots of sharp angles.

Betty Joel set up a company with her husband in 1919 and produced simple functional pieces that were also sophisticated, in a style that was closest to the luxurious Modernism of Printz or Frank. Many of her commissions were for decorative schemes for hotels, shops and offices. She also produced inexpensive easy-care furniture for the modern working woman and influenced the cheaper end of the market, which copied many of her designs. The designer and decorator Syrie Maugham helped to promote a glamorous Hollywood-style modernistic Deco that became popular in the 1930s; a fashion for mirror, glass and chromium plating everywhere, deep carpets in abstract designs and minimalist furniture. She was particularly known for her all-white schemes. Mirrored and glass furniture became all the rage, and lent a dramatically glittering note to sober interiors, amplifying the sense of space and light. Mirror was particularly associated with the ubiquitous cocktail cabinet.

A remarkable furniture designer of this period was Denham MacLaren although he remained relatively obscure, partly because of his small output. Using all the standard materials of modernistic Deco, including glass and plated tubing, he invented highly unusual and sophisticated pieces.

In Finland the Modernist architect Alvar Aalto initiated serial production furniture and in 1931 established a firm in Helsinki, Artek, which manufactured furniture, lighting fixtures and fabrics in a Bauhaus style adapted to traditional materials and designs.

Elsewhere in Scandinavia, particularly in Sweden, a strong style emerged in the late 1920s, influenced by Bauhaus functionalism. Lightweight, practical, simple shapes were set in airy Modernist spaces. Bruno Mathsson was the best known of the Swedish designers and his very successful line of bent and laminated wood furniture was designed with comfort as well as function in mind. The architect Erik Gunnar Asplund developed a style that blended Modernist with classicist tendencies.

Opposite: Bathroom of Claridges Hotel, fitted in modernistic Deco style, London, 1930s.

3
TEXTILES

Opposite: *'La Danse'* block-printed repeating fabric design, c.
1910, by Raoul Dufy, who drew on eighteenth-century examples
in his work.

Until the Art Deco period textile manufacturers were still running through the deadly repertoire of period designs. General developments in the decorative arts and the changing aspect of the modern interior, however, divorced textiles from conventional designs and conventional attitudes to the role they should play in an interior. This was a discipline in which women were particularly prominent.

Paul Poiret, who played such an important role in the development of a modern French style in furniture and interior decoration was equally involved in liberating textiles from their dependency on past styles. The girls in his Atelier Martine produced bright, colorful, naive designs based on observations of nature, the best of which were transposed onto fabrics, wallpapers and carpets. Poiret conceived of a new style of decorating in which simple geometrical furniture was set against walls and floors that were covered in these vibrant designs. Inspired by the décors created by Léon Bakst and others for the Ballets Russes, he jumbled patterns, colors and luxuriant satiny fabrics for a rich exotic flavor. Although the fashion for this elaborate decorative chaos was short-lived, the effect of warm and lively textile designs juxtaposed with relatively plain pieces

of furniture, was one sought by the majority of Art Deco decorators.

In most interiors of the high Art Deco period (up to the mid-1920s), walls and floors were covered with complex patterns that repeated the standard repertoire of Deco motifs and provided a rich surface covering as well as a unifying element in a room. A liking for the Atelier Martine pattern-on-pattern effect lingered on, with inlay and marquetry designs on furniture set against patterned carpets and wallpapers.

It was clear at the 1925 Exposition that the textile industry was lagging behind the other decorative arts in the quest for modernity, and was too reliant on traditional designs, and too pictorial. Eventually, as furniture became plainer, the role of textiles grew increasingly important. In overall patterned environments the clean forms of exquisite pieces of furniture were set off to advantage. Ruhlmann always used pattern to contrast with simple pieces of furniture and to unify an *ensemble*.

In the context of Modernism and Le Corbusier's insistence that walls should be white and unadorned, textiles became one of the few decorative accents (or even the only one) in otherwise rather austere interiors, and designers came to see the role of textiles as providing the main source of warmth, color and pattern in a

Below left: *'Les Cactus'* wallpaper design by Atelier Martine.

Below right: Louis Marcoussis's carpet, c. 1926, was bought by Jacques Doucet for his studio at Neuilly.

Left: Tapestry, c. 1927, by Gunta Stadler-Stölzl, whose Bauhaus workshop was extremely influential in its radical approach.

room. They also began to make use of new synthetic materials together with new methods of production.

Walls became plainer, carpets shrank in size, patterns were less hectic and obtrusive, and color schemes were either subtle and muted or based on a single primary color. At the Bau-

haus Gunta Stadler-Stölzl ran an important weaving workshop and encouraged experimentation with weaving techniques and use of new materials. The Bauhaus workshop exercised a massive influence in its liberation of color, its abolition of conventional decoration and the generally fresh approach it took to tex-

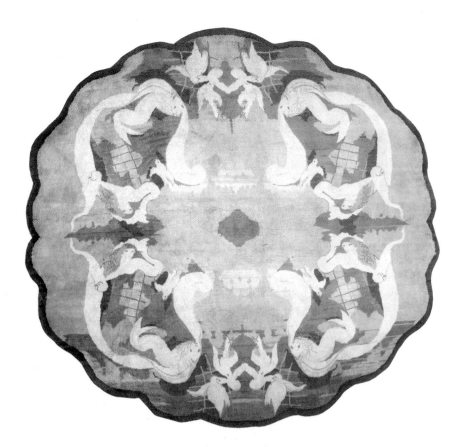

Above: Marie Laurencin's tufted wool carpet, 1934, is reminiscent of her paintings (page 161).

tile design. In France too there was a move towards using synthetic fibres and exploiting varying techniques of production, in order to create textural effects and abstract patterns.

In common with the other disciplines of the decorative arts, textile design drew inspiration from a range of sources including Cubism, primitive arts, Oriental and Middle Eastern art. There was a basic progression from dense florid designs to abstract geometrical ones.

Most of the great *ensembliers* involved themselves in the design of textiles: Maurice Dufrène, Emile-Jacques Ruhlmann, Süe et Mare, Eileen Gray, Paul Follot and Francis Jourdain, to name a few of the best known. They recognized that textiles were not a casual addition to an *ensemble* but needed to be carefully integrated. Eileen Gray, for example, clearly took as much care in the design and placing of her rugs as she did with any piece of furniture.

Carpets and fabrics of the Art Deco period have not survived well to the present. Textiles are by nature ephemeral – they fade and wear out, making it difficult to give an exact assessment of the output of any period. Fortunately numerous photographs and colored albums of designs help to fill this gap.

CARPETS

In the high Deco phase carpets were large (often wall-to-wall), highly decorative and colorful. Designs were generally floral and fruity, in the French tradition; Dufrène, Groult, Follot, Ruhlmann and Süe et Mare all designed knotted carpets patterned with flowers. Marie

Laurencin was an exception in this group, for she applied themes recurrent in her paintings – young girls and animals in soft pastel colors – to the carpets she designed. Several carpet manufacturers, perceiving that the developments in design were becoming popular, commissioned work from well-known Deco artists such as Follot, Süe et Mare and Robert Bonfils.

Ivan da Silva Bruhns was the greatest of the French rug designers of the period, and the designer who first applied a modern approach to the medium. As was true of all artists who revolutionized design in their different fields, he took a great interest in craftsmanship and materials, and even developed a variant of the traditional knotted stitch. He was equally concerned with the function of a carpet in an *ensemble* and developed his style in keeping with the tendency to simplify and geometricize. He marketed his own designs and provided carpets for a number of *ensembliers*. His early carpets incorporate motifs such as the key pattern borrowed from Greek art. He was also strongly influenced by Berber designs and techniques of rugmaking which he would have known from the exhibitions of Moroccan art held in Paris from around 1915. He worked in deep, rich, earthy tones, reminiscent of the natural dye colors of Berber rugs. In later years his designs became more abstract, incorporating a Cubist application of overlapping geometrical shapes which he often interspersed with rows of dots or notches.

When Doucet was furnishing his Neuilly studio he commissioned carpet designs from the painter Louis Marcoussis and adapted cartoons by the sculptor Gustav Miklos. They both worked in a dramatic Cubist-inspired style setting a precedent in Modernist carpet design.

Eileen Gray also pioneered a simple abstract style of carpet design which she sold with the furniture from her shop, Jean Désert. These were small rugs with deep luxurious piles and bold abstract designs. Some were quite loosely woven and textured to contrast with glossy lacquered surfaces. Carpets in her *ensembles* always had a very precise function. In the interior she designed for Suzanne Talbot she repeated on the carpets the motifs that decorated the walls, so that the furniture seemed to float in an environment of swirling shapes. Elsewhere rugs were designed and placed to draw together the different elements in a room, and as such played a role both focal and dramatic.

In Modernist interiors carpets became important additions to the setting, providing color, warmth and a note of individuality in the midst of all the near-identical tubular furniture. As if the carpet had risen in status and was now asserting its importance in the general scheme of a room, designs grew large, bold and also sculptural, with patterns cut into the pile in relief, and an emphasis on texture. At the same time carpets shrank in size, and furniture was arranged around and over it to create interesting sculptural juxtapositions. Carpets were frequently used to accent architectural features or emphasize spatial play; Chareau, for example, placed a round carpet by Jean Lurçat beneath the cupola of his study-library in the Ambassade Française at the 1925 Exposition.

A number of good carpet designs came out of England during this period, most of them designed by women. Betty Joel used Da Silva Bruhn's rugs in her interiors for a time, then began to design her own. These were simple and understated, often in creamy tones.

The graphic designer Edward McKnight Kauffer and his wife Marion Dorn were both successful designers of avant-garde hand-knotted carpets, though Dorn was the more brilliant. She made carpet design her specialization and developed a technique of cutting the pile to create interesting textural patterns. Kauffer's rugs were decorated with bold geometrical patterns and were often used by the decorators Raymond McGrath and David Pleydell-Bouverie in their interiors.

WALLPAPER AND FABRICS

The high Deco style in wallpaper, as typified by Süe et Mare's *ensembles*, was a lush all-over covering of flowers and fruit within a geometrical framework, a grid or a trellis. Emphasis was on color combinations. André Groult was influential in commissioning designs for block-printed cloth from other artists for use in his interiors. Ruhlmann applied bold, over-scaled, repeating designs to his walls and upholstery.

Many *ensembliers* designed large ranges of different textiles and printed papers to complement their interiors, and the Parisian department stores produced various light Deco and, later, modernistic designs to go with their furniture. Pictorial compositions of contemporary *fête champêtres* designed by André

Above: Hand-knotted wool carpet, c. 1930-33, by Ivan da Silva Bruhns, most innovative of the French designers.

Below: Axminster rug, c. 1925, designed by Edward McKnight Kauffer.

Left: Tapestry wall-hanging, 1921, by Marianne Geyer-Pankok; in Eastern Europe, traditional folk art was blended with Deco influences.

Mare, André Marty and Charles Martin were frequently printed up as room hangings or made into screens.

Not surprisingly, tapestry upholstery was popular with the traditionalist designers and enjoyed a revival during this period. The French had an enduring reputation as great tapestry masters, but standards had rather fallen in the nineteenth century, with a wealth of second-rate pictorial designs dominating output. By the 1920s most of the large decorating firms and department stores were marketing screens and seat furniture upholstered in tap-

estry. A number of tapestry manufacturers of long standing, such as Aubusson, La Manufacture Nationale de Tapis et Couverts de Beauvais and La Manufacture Nationale de Gobelins, retained their own design team. Jean Lurçat worked for Aubusson in the 1930s and succeeded in singlehandedly reviving the art of tapestry by applying geometrical designs and creating compositions that focused on the interplay of colors or on textural contrasts. Chareau used Lurçat's tapestry designs to upholster his furniture. But the old habit of reproducing contemporary paintings in tapestry

lived on; in the late 1920s and 1930s Marie Cuttoli, who worked for Aubusson, commissioned major artists such as Matisse, Picasso and Léger to design tapestry cartoons. On the whole, however, the results were too painterly and therefore inappropriate to the medium, and did not achieve great success.

One of Poiret's protégés, Raoul Dufy, was an inspired fabric designer as well as a painter and graphic artist. His designs were influenced by the narrative eighteenth-century style, with small but elaborate repeating scenes of fishermen, tennis-players and dancers. He also designed the standard decorative fruit and floral fabrics and papers. From 1912 to 1928 he worked for the Bianchini-Férier textile company. He exhibited wall hangings in Poiret's barges at the 1925 Exposition featuring fashionable ladies in fashionable locations: at the races, the casino, a regatta. The example Dufy set by involving himself with textile design encouraged many young designers to contribute to the revival of the industry and the craft.

Below: Fabric by Hélène Henri woven with geometrical motifs.

Sonia Delaunay was another of the leading fabric designers of the period. She worked in a dynamic geometrical style, creating abstract patterns in mainly primary colors which were based on a variant of Cubism called Simultaneism which she and her husband had developed. In the years before World War I she became interested in fabric design through experiments with color relationships and juxtapositions. Her work was much imitated and began a fashion for contrasting color schemes. Her dress fabrics were always conceived with a view to the appearance of the pattern when worn and the way they might complement the movement of the wearer.

The Modernists, led by Le Corbusier, declared war on wallpaper. In the late 1920s the taste for bright color schemes waned and in its place came a fashion for subdued, earthy, neutral tones which lasted through the early years of the Depression. This shift in emphasis was accompanied by the abandonment of printed fabrics and a concentration on the textures of woven fabric. In France Hélène Henri, founder member of the UAM (Union des Artistes Modernes), set up a craft-weaving workshop in the early 1920s and became the chief exponent of this new style, which owed much to the influence of the Bauhaus. The raw material was exalted and new synthetic fibres incorporated; rayon and cellulose among others. There was no need for printed decoration. Good weaving, it was felt, was beautiful in itself; varieties of weaves were explored and unusual materials such as straw were woven into the fabric for interesting textural effects. Heavy upholstery materials such as tweed contrasted well with metal frames. Hélène Henri's fabrics became very fashionable and were used by Mallet-Stevens, Jourdain and Chareau among others. Her designs were based on thick weave plaids and stripes, or repeating geometrical motifs in neutral tones. Designers like Jean-Michel Frank covered walls in plain textured fabrics, vellum or suede.

The Omega group take much credit for revolutionizing printed fabrics in England, and introducing abstract and geometrical designs, although the effect on the textile industry was delayed until long after the war. Just as British furniture design remained largely unaffected by the developments in France, so too did textile design languish until the late 1920s.

William Foxton, owner of a textile company, was one of the few who fed good designs by talented artists into the textile industry. In the 1920s he sought out designers capable of creating an exciting modern idiom for fabric design. The stark silhouetted angularity of Vorticism translated particularly well as a decorative style, and many dynamic and interesting abstract patterns were produced.

Another important contribution to English textile design was made by the Phyllis Baron and Dorothy Larcher partnership. They concentrated on block-printed fabrics, both updated floral chintz-types and bold geometrical designs. They specialized in the Indian method of bleaching a pattern onto a colored ground, known as discharge printing. Later on they were joined by Enid Marx, a talented artist who designed an extremely successful range of upholstery fabric for the London Passenger Transport Board. Marion Dorn was better known for her sculpted carpets but she also produced some simple inexpensive fabric designs for the old Bleach Linen Co. Ltd for which she, with Paul Nash, was principal designer.

In around 1910 the Wiener Werkstätte had established a separate textile division to provide carpets and fabrics for specific interiors. The results were so successful that the workshop was enlarged and an independent retail outlet established in 1917. Early textiles designed by Koloman Moser and Josef Hoffmann were austere – rigidly geometrical with monochrome checks and herringbone patterns. From the late 1910s, however, bright color and lively decorative motifs began to creep into their designs. Dagobert Peche was one of the most brilliant of the later designers, working in a style that was based on Austrian baroque and rococo motifs.

A group of designers in Germany produced designs more akin to Deco than to the Bauhaus work. Marie Hannich, for instance, applied angular geometrical renderings of images of

ships, cars and buildings to fabrics. Textile design in Denmark, Belgium and Scandinavia was modernized along similar lines. Traditional forms of weaving were combined with folk or primitive designs that were angularized and applied alongside geometrical ornament. In Russia bright textiles and wallpapers incorporating abstract geometrical designs – some rather alarmingly exuberant – were designed by avant-garde artists such as Varvara Stefanova and Liubov Popova, as part of the general attempt to create a totally new idiom.

Above: Printed linen, 1922, by Gregory Brown for William Foxton.

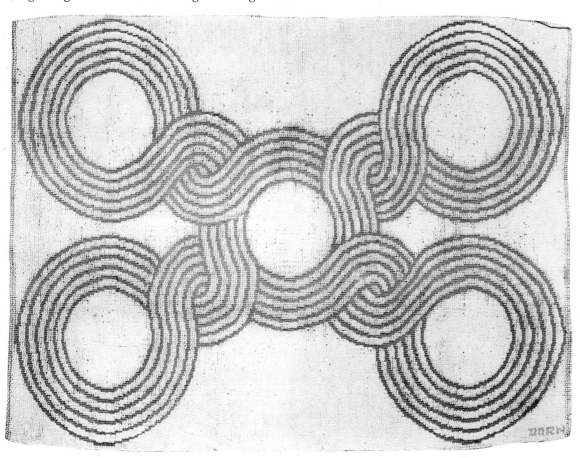

Left: Woven carpet, c. 1935, by Marion Dorn.

4
METALWORK

Metalwork of the Art Deco period was particularly strongly dominated by Parisian design. The output of the period is not easy to characterize, yet this much can be said of all the best work, from the magnificent wrought-iron creations of Brandt to the simple hammered metal pots of Linossier: that there is a consistency of approach, a sensitivity to the metal, and an exploitation of its properties for decorative ends.

During the nineteenth century French ironwork had given up trying to compete with the obvious economic advantages of foundry work and had gradually gone into decline. The great Art Nouveau designers Guimard and Majorelle had certainly contributed to the renaissance of the craft of the *ferronier*, but at the turn of the century the industry was still enfeebled and iron was cast into the most insensitive historical plagiarisms. By the 1920s the craft was fully revived and modernized, and beginning to win back the reputation it had earned for itself in the eighteenth century.

Its great versatility made ironwork suitable for adaptation to modern design; it could be made to appear massive and crude or delicate and refined. Various patinas could be applied to its surface and iron could be combined with other metals such as brass, copper, steel and aluminum. Recent scientific advances in the field of metallurgy had shown that there was enormous potential for varying treatments and methods of production. As long as the designer was skilful and imaginative, there were endless design possibilities. Once ironwork had regained its popularity a wide variety of objects

Right: Girault shopfront, Paris, c. 1925 (Azema, Edrei and Hardy, architects); an example of the ornate ironwork that was applied to façades in the early Deco period.

became available, from jewelry and small objects to monumental architectural features.

The new atmosphere of daring and innovation in design encouraged decorators and ironworkers to rethink the role of iron and other metals in an interior. A single piece of ironwork as a focus to a room was always successful; it added an element of precision and monumentality. Console tables topped by a richly grained slab of marble were popular, as were screens, chandeliers, mirror frames and firedogs in iron. With the advent of modern conveniences in homes and offices, ironwork acquired new roles. The ugly radiators that were a necessary adjunct of central heating installations could be disguised with ironwork screens, which neither disturbed the air flow nor were damaged by the heat. In new apart-ment and office blocks ironwork lift cages were installed, often highly decorative and designed to match balustrades and entrance doors. Ironwork was also imaginatively applied to the exteriors of buildings: balconies, grilles, and particularly shop-fronts. Decorative screens backed in glass became very popular as shop doors, and designs were often extended to frame windows and incorporate lettering cut or cast in iron, presenting a unified and distinctive façade. As modern buildings became more austere, ironwork was often the only element of decorative relief on a façade.

The high Art Deco style with its stylized motifs – sunbursts, fountains, doves, gazelles and endless floral fantasies – adapted well to ironwork. When the style matured and these motifs were replaced by more rigorous abstract

Left: Entrance doors of the Maison Paul Poiret on the Champs Elysées in Paris, with metalwork by Edgar Brandt, c. 1925.

forms, ironwork was versatile enough to adapt but other metals more suitable to the expression of that style also came into their own.

Much of the credit for the highly successful revival of wrought-iron goes to Edgar Brandt, undisputedly the leading exponent of the period. His technical mastery of the material and his exploitation of the various properties of the metals he worked with, earned him this unrivaled reputation. In the interest of achieving new decorative effects, he varied color, tone and patina and in later years experimented with combinations of metals, using new alloys such as 'Studal' and steel as well as aluminum to create striking contrasts. He developed tech-

niques which allowed him to present a highly finished appearance and to disguise the methods of construction. He also perfected a virtually invisible seaming technique known as autogenous welding that gave his work a particularly smooth finish. He often worked in close association with other designers and artisans, and was always prepared to execute other people's designs. Brandt was not a craftsman who jealously protected and promoted handcrafted work and he used industrial techniques whenever it was possible to do so, in order to cut corners without jeopardizing the quality of the finished product. He used stamping presses, for instance, to repeat patterns.

Brandt's work was essentially in the high Art Deco tradition, incorporating most of the characteristic motifs of that period in a characteristically mannered and refined style. He worked the iron into deceptively fluid, delicate and graceful forms based on scrolls and flowers. His many public commissions for buildings and monuments, as well as collaborative projects with architects and interior designers and private commissions for homes and hotels, required him to design and execute shelving systems, room dividers, radiator covers, fire screens, lamps, stair rails and balconies.

In the early 1920s Brandt opened a showroom in Paris where he exhibited glassware, ceramics, jewelry and other crafts which complemented his designs, alongside his own ware. One of his most successful pieces was the serpent standard lamp with alabaster or glass shade, called 'La Tentation'. From as early as 1910, Brandt formed an association with the Daum glassworks. They provided glass shades, often acid-etched or smooth and opaque, for his wrought-iron supports and fixtures.

As for many of the best Art Deco designers, the Paris Exposition was the making of Brandt's career. He exhibited widely, but his most significant contributions were the Porte d'Honneur – the main entrance to the exhibition – and the five-paneled 'Oasis' screen. His gift for successfully applying decoration to a monumental work was clearly demonstrated in the massive gateway, which he designed in collaboration with André Ventre and Henri Favier. A grille of repeating fountain motifs linked groups of columns topped by more stylized fountains. The project was also a measure of Brandt's technical skill, for it was an achievement in itself to succeed in endowing the cheap alloy 'staff' with the qualities of a more noble metal. Brandt also provided objects and furniture for Ruhlmann's pavilion at the exhibition, and furnished his own pavilion in ironwork throughout. The Oasis screen was the *pièce de résistance*; it is more angular in style than Brandt's early work, and large chevron-patterned leaves are a striking element of the design. A streamlined fountain flows against a background of these large variegated leaves in iron and brass. After the Exposition, Brandt became a designer of international repute. By 1926 he had established overseas showrooms in New York and London.

Like Brandt, Raymond Subes was apprenticed to the great Art Nouveau ironsmith Emile Robert and, like Brandt, he was extremely prolific. Subes' technique was much simpler, however, and was popular because he achieved rich and elegant decorative effects at relatively low cost. He also explored new techniques and in particular methods of industrial production which he applied to his designs for both furniture and monumental architectural pieces. Whenever he could do so without sacrificing the quality of hand-crafted pieces, he used machines to ease his work, mainly for cutting and polishing. Subes contributed to the general advance toward Modernist ideals by striving to

maintain artistic quality as well as to make pieces easy and cheap to produce, and by incorporating industrial techniques which for too long had been anathema to designers. His style evolved alongside the general development of Art Deco; in the early 1920s he was working in a very delicate scrolled style, while

Above: Wrought-iron fire screen, early 1920s, by Edgar Brandt, master of Deco metalwork.

Below: Raymond Subes's console table in wrought-iron and marble, c. 1925, is typical of his simpler more delicate style.

Right: Edgar Brandt's interior panel of a lift cage for the new entrance loggia of Selfridges department store, London. The panel was adapted from a design of 1922 entitled *Les Cigognes d'Alsace.*

his exhibits at the 1925 Exposition show that he was moving towards a decorative idiom that was more angular and less elaborate. He finally evolved the fully Modernist mode, developing an exceptionally strong geometrical style. Like Brandt he worked mostly in wrought-iron, which he occasionally combined with bronze or copper and, in later years, with steel and aluminum.

Various other wrought-iron masters deserve

mention. Paul Kiss was a Romanian who settled in France and collaborated for a while with Brandt and his work displays a similarly lyrical quality. He worked in a distinctive style that combined angular forms with floral and scrolled motifs. His work was distinguished by its *martelé* decoration, a treatment that involved hammering deep incisions into the metal.

The Nics *frères* company was formed by two Hungarian-born brothers who had settled in Paris. They designed and crafted a wide range of decorative ironwork, mostly architectural but also some furniture. They gave their work a hammered finish, and developed a simple angular style.

Bronze was Rateau's metal; its archaic-looking greenish patina complemented his designs, and the skill required to work it made it an expensive luxury, in keeping with the refinement and exclusivity of Rateau's interiors. Bronze was previously the preserve of locksmiths, and Rateau was responsible for reviving its use in furniture.

Fontaine et Cie were a Parisian firm who were bold enough to take on all kinds of commissions in the decorative hardware line from fashionable Deco designers. Süe et Mare used them a great deal to execute designs for clocks, mirrors and light fixtures in their characteristic

floral style. Maurice Dufrène also had a taste for ironwork and used Fontaine et Cie for his designs, including a dining room in wrought-iron

Above: Edgar Brandt's *Oasis* five-paneled screen in wrought-iron and gilt-bronze, made in collaboration with Henri Favier and featured as one of the prime exhibits at the 1925 Exposition.

Left: Raymond Subes's stainless steel grill, set with cabochons of Lalique glass.

Right: Lacquered vase decorated with crushed eggshell, 1923-24, by Jean Dunand.

Far right: Hammered and chased nickel-silver vase inlaid with silver, 1926, by Claudius Linossier.

Below: Enameled copper vase, c. 1925, by Camille Fauré.

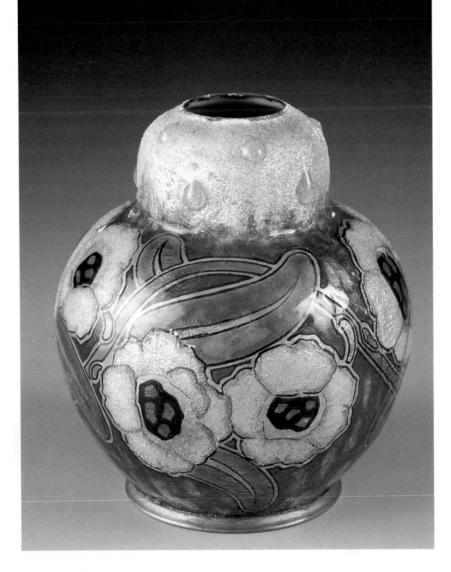

and glass, the table supported by a clever system of curved metal ribbons.

As the streamlined modernistic look took over from high Art Deco, new alloys began to replace the more traditional metals. These were lighter and cheaper to produce without being any less strong. Highly polished tubular metals were used architecturally, most typically in the form of railings which accentuated the horizontal lines of a building and were often the only decorative element on a façade.

The development of steel tubing allowed furniture designers to create a new idiom; light frames, smooth surfaces and neat forms. Much of this tubing was chromium or nickel plated, with a glossy reflective finish that distinguishes Deco furniture from the severe functionalist designs of the Modernists.

The abundant ironwork flourishes on shopfronts were replaced by neater, starker, but no less distinctive designs in metal and glass. Mallet-Stevens clad the façade of the Bally shoe shop in riveted plates of brass. Other shop fronts were totally plain except for the lettering that ran across the façade in a three-dimensional design cut from sheet metal.

In Britain, the fancy high Parisian style of metalwork was adopted, but it was cheaply reproduced and was generally used to decorate cinemas and hotels.

DINANDERIE AND ENAMEL

Dinanderie is the name given to the art of hand working objects from non-precious metals, usually by hammering. A single sheet of metal, usually copper, lead or pewter, is teased into a vase, platter or bowl form with infinite skill and patience. The metal has to be constantly reheated to make it soft and malleable, and a variety of tools has to be used, working inside and out, to shape the metal and control its spread. The revival of dinanderie work owed much to the great surge of interest in Japanese art.

What is characteristic of the work of the artists who specialized in dinanderie is their sensitivity to the materials and their skill as craftsmen. Although many of their pieces were decorated, it was the tone and surface treatment of the metals that assumed prime importance, and articles were lovingly fashioned, with all the potential for contrast between shadow and reflected light fully exploited.

The decoration of these objects is equally painstaking work. Patinas are achieved by applying acids, metal oxides and a naked flame. Sometimes the surface is carved or chased, or else is inlaid with other metals. This involves grooving out a design, then filling it with a plug of softer metal and hammering it into place. A pleasing effect is achieved if the two metals are then heated so that they fuse into one another slightly and the tones mingle and become smoky.

Jean Dunand was the grand master of dinanderie. He grew up in Geneva, and in 1896 won a scholarship and came to Paris to study sculpture. He became apprenticed to the sculptor Jean Dampt, who was an admirer of the English Arts and Crafts movement. Under Dampt's influence he began gradually to abandon sculpture and became a metalworker, handcrafting his pieces in the most arduous fashion. In the early years of the century he was exhibiting works in a late Art Nouveau style, rather overblown and not at all true to his real taste, which eventually led him to create plainer forms. He abandoned these bulbous organic shapes and after 1918 concentrated on abstract patterns which he applied to enhance forms. His best work is very simple and elegant, a marriage of Oriental, African and traditional influences; round gourd-shaped or elongated vases, the surfaces worked with patinas, chiseling and overlays in gold and silver and decorated with abstract incrustations. He worked in a variety of metals including lead, nickel and steel. In his later work he abandoned decoration altogether and concentrated on creating pure forms, absolutely plain except for a very striking lacquered finish in brilliant color, mostly blacks, reds and golds.

Once he had mastered the technique of lacquering Dunand began to apply lacquer to his hammered metal forms. He fully exploited the technique of *coquille d'oeuf* (the application of fragments of eggshell) for its decorative potential. With all the possible gradations in tone and texture, in combination with gold and silver leaf and different colored lacquers that this technique offered, Dunand was kept busy devising a seemingly limitless repertoire of decorative treatments for his dinanderie. He became so absorbed with lacquerwork that he gave up metalwork to concentrate on creating largescale lacquer designs and also lacquered furniture.

Left: Jean Dunand's hammered copper vase, gilded and patinated, early 1920s.

Below: English silver and enamel cigarette case, c. 1931.

The other important master of dinanderie of this period was Claudius Linossier, who worked chiefly in copper. His work is subtle and understated, its abstract ornament derived from ancient art forms, the metal inlays expanded and fused into one another to create smoky, shimmering tones. Linossier's admiration for Etruscan pottery led him to experiment with metal incrustation, which became his speciality. He was also concerned with enriching surface texture, by creating special alloys with unusual tonal effects or by burnishing the metals, though he rarely tried to disguise the rough unpatinated surface of copper.

Maurice Daurat worked exclusively in pewter, experimenting with form and with treatments that would enhance the soft, ductile, heavy quality of the metal. His forms were pure with an absolute minimum of decoration.

Elsewhere in Europe the German firm Würtembergische Metallwarenfabrik, who were most famous for their Jugendstil objects, adapted the Parisian Art Deco style in the 1920s and produced a successful range of metalwork objects in a light, rather stereotyped decorative style, not nearly as sensitive as the work of the French metalworkers. At the Bauhaus in the 1920s, Wilhelm Wagenfeld was designing metal objects in a rather futuristic style. Marianne Brandt was the greatest German metalworker of the period, however; she joined the Bauhaus in 1924 and became renowned for her

Left: Lettering on a shopfront by René Herbst.

metal lamps. Like the silversmith Jean Puiforcat, she adhered to geometrical principles in her work.

Jean Goulden and Camille Fauré were the chief exponents of enamelwork in the Art Deco period. Goulden became fascinated by Byzantine enamelwork while staying in a Greek monastery on Mount Athos on his way home from foreign service during World War I. When he returned to France he learned the champlevé enameling technique from Jean Dunand. He worked in silver, gilded copper and bronze and his designs were rigorously geometrical, displaying the influence of Cubism. He created clocks, lampstands, candlesticks and other objects in bronze and enamel: sculptural, asymetrical compositions made up of irregular, overlapping geometrical forms. He also made boxes with compositions of triangles, circles and zigzags, sometimes with sections applied in relief.

Enamel is made by combining powdered glass with chemical pigments and fusing it to a metal base. Limoges was traditionally famous for its enamels and Camille Fauré set up his workshop in Limoges. Working on a copper ground he created colorful enamel vases, decorated with geometrical motifs, thickly sculpted in relief and in pastel color combinations. His early work was more richly colored and floral.

Below: The Citroën showroom in Amsterdam, c. 1930 (Jan Wils, architect). The runged balustrade is used to add emphasis to the horizontal lines of the building, and to provide a decorative flourish in a relatively austere interior.

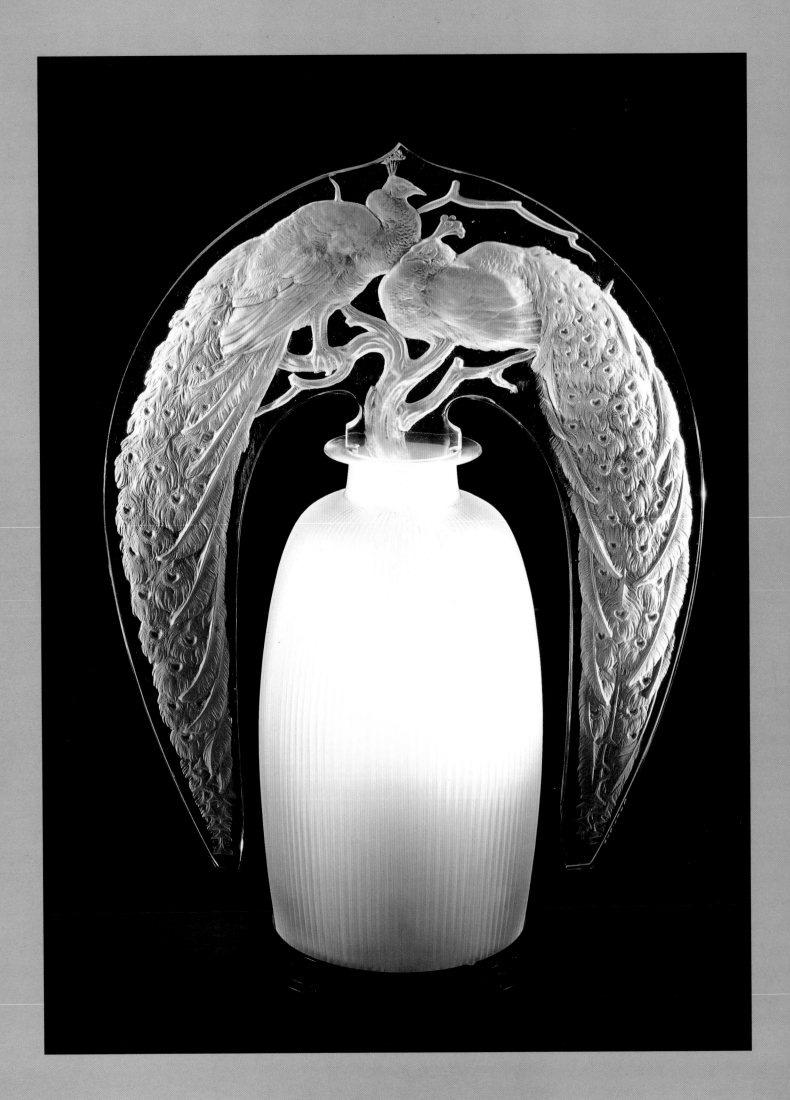

5
LIGHTING

There was a steady increase through the 1920s and 1930s in the number of people who had electricity in their homes. Electric light first came into use in the last years of the nineteenth century. By the Art Deco period it was no longer a recent invention, but it was some time before it was reliable and cheap enough to become ubiquitous, and even by the mid-1930s electricity was by no means a feature of every home. Once the system had been perfected the advantages of electric light were enormous, for it was brighter, cleaner, less hazardous, more versatile in its applications and far easier to use.

Yet it took some time before electricity was fully exploited for its lighting capacity, and designs for lighting fixtures displayed a search for maximum efficiency. Lamps were either designed in imitation of the old gas and candle fixtures or else were decorative, highly colored creations, sometimes fashioned into animal shapes and emitting only a very soft filtered glow. Designers were more concerned with magic lantern effects than with lighting rooms and banishing the gloom of centuries. In either case the tendency was to disguise the electric fittings as far as possible.

When designers finally moved away from the attractions of colored light, they began to realize the true potential of electric lighting. The gradual assimilation of electricity into daily life coincided with the period of intense creative activity in the decorative arts during the interwar period. Thus *ensembliers*, metal

Below: Wrought-iron chandelier with alabaster shades, by Edgar Brandt.

and glassworkers, and artists from other fields of design were drawn to explore the decorative as well as the practical applications of electric lighting, and to assign it an important role in the modern interior. Lighting became a serious concern, and competitions and Salons of Light were held frequently through the 1920s and 1930s to stimulate new ideas in design.

Great care was always taken to eliminate any aggressive glare and to break up ugly points of light. Translucent materials such as parchment, alabaster and sand-blasted or thickly molded glass were found to filter a milky diffused quality of light that was not harsh on the eyes. The revolution in lighting began with experiments; shallow basins of thick glass or alabaster were suspended by a system of cords or chains from the ceiling to replace the redundant multi-armed candelabra form and the imitation candles. The idea of lighting from a central hanging fixture and from wall brackets remained dominant for some time.

Although the functional nature of lighting was becoming more important, lamps and light fixtures continued to be regarded as highly decorative *objets d'art*, and few designers could resist their potential for decorative effect. In an interior, the light source was frequently the most unusual and in some ways the dominant feature. This went on being true even of the most modernistic interiors of the late 1920s and early 1930s.

The marriage of wrought-iron and glass in designs for light fixtures was a highly successful one, and continued to be popular through to the mid-1920s, when it was superseded by plainer, less unwieldy designs. The weight and strength of iron contrasted well with the fragility of glass. Designs were very decorative, in the scrolled and floral manner favored by the wrought-iron masters. Lamps of glass blown into a wrought-iron armature and often made up into animal shapes were a particular fashion of the period. Their effect when lit was of pure light trapped in an iron mesh.

Edgar Brandt was producing iron *torchères* and wall sconces from early on in his career and around 1910 he formed an association with the glass manufacturers Daum. His rearing serpent standard lamp, complete with early Daum shade in a marble effect of swirling color, was extremely popular and was sold in three sizes. Later on, when Daum was concentrating on heavier glassware etched with floral or geometrical designs in grainy and smooth textures, the style was still strong enough to complement Brandt's designs; and often the decorative motifs of the armature were repeated in the acid-etched design of the shade. Brandt did not exclusively use Daum glass, and on occasion worked with Lalique and other manufacturers, but his work was particularly well suited to Daum's glass designs.

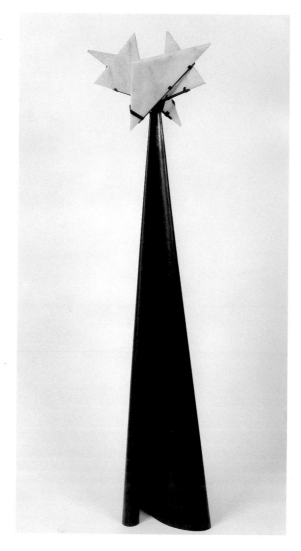

In addition to producing glass shades for the wrought-iron masters, the Daum firm also manufactured an innovative range of glass lamps of their own design. Many of these were cast in mushroom or cylindrical shapes; the glass was thick, generally in white and creamy tints, and acid-etched with strong geometrical designs. Sometimes a matching base was illuminated from within. Metal mounts were almost invisible and forms strong and sculptural.

Albert Cheuret specialized in unusual and exotic Art Deco lamps, often in animal forms and in a style inspired by Antiquity. Mounts were generally in bronze, and set with thin slices of alabaster. Rateau also produced a range of lamps in bronze which incorporated the highly individual animal motifs that adorned his furniture and interiors.

The lighting of glass, and its potential for decorative effect, was a great stimulus to René Lalique's fantasy and inventiveness. From around 1914 he began to explore the possibilities of lighting glass electrically, and was one of the first to hit upon the idea of suspending a simple shallow bowl or globe from the ceiling. These he molded in characteristic stylized designs – fruit, flowers, fish and birds – which stood out in relief against the diffused glow of the thick opalescent background, most of the

light being reflected off the ceiling. Sometimes he added a flattering pastel tint, or colored the glass to harmonize with a particular decor. Often decorative motifs matched wall sconces and even tableware. An extension of the idea of suspending a single basin was to hang a series of basins of decreasing size from the ceiling, one above the other, so that the light thrown upwards from each basin illuminated the moldings or etched decorations of those above. This was an intelligent and effective substitute for the chandelier. Lalique also developed the idea of applying molded glass cornices around a room which concealed electric bulbs and cast an overall diffused light. He used a similar device in his decorative scheme for Maples furniture store in the Tottenham Court Road, London. The firm of Genet and Michon, who specialized in lighting fixtures, were the originators of this idea and manufactured illuminated press-molded glass panels that ran around a room like a cornice or could be placed against walls and ceilings.

Lalique's lighting designs undoubtedly made him more sensitive to the way light could enhance glass: its effect on molding, color, etched decoration and varying thicknesses and textures of glass. He designed a series of *sur-touts-de-table*, decorative objects with the light

Above left: Pierre Chareau's Cubist-inspired *La Religieuse* lamp, with metal standard and shade made up of sections of alabaster, 1923.

Above: Edgar Brandt's wrought iron chandelier, with etched glass shades by Daum, c. 1925. Brandt worked in association with the glass manufacturers Daum from about 1910.

Right: Glass table lamp with illuminated base, c. 1925, by Daum, one of their innovative range of glass lamps.

Far right: René Lalique's glass chandelier with molded mistletoe design.

Below: Pair of gilt-bronze *La Tentation* floor lamps with Daum shades, early 1920s, by Edgar Brandt.

source concealed in a bronze base and thrown upwards on to delicate semicircular sheets of glass etched with peacocks, swallows, or a firebird design inspired by Stravinsky's ballet of the same name. These were developed from his glass *luminaires* lamps – illuminated vases sprouting etched bouquets. He also created illuminated ceilings, fountains and tables. Although his glass was never cheap, Lalique designed for large-series production and many of his wares were exported abroad, particularly to England. By the early 1930s his light fittings were almost a cliché of the contemporary interior, in London as much as in Paris.

Ruhlmann designed monumental lighting fixtures and was particularly fond of the urn shape which thrust the light upwards, emphasizing the height of ceilings. He also hung massive chandeliers made up of crystal beads strung together in cascading rivulets. These were quite a feature of the high Deco interior and remained popular through the 1930s. Süe et Mare produced a range of table lamps and wall fixtures, which were most often molded in the flowers-and-fruit relief that adorned so many of their pieces. Many of the artists who worked in *pâte-de-verre*, such as Gabriel Argy-Rousseau and Alméric Walter, produced small sculptured lamps and wall lights in relatively large quantities. The deep colors and translucent quality of the glass made them pretty decorative additions to a room.

Many of the designers who adopted a more modernistic idiom were instrumental in freeing lighting design from its archaic and anachronistic forms and giving it a new importance in decorative schemes. In his capacity both as architect and decorator, Pierre Chareau was particularly sensitive to every aspect of lighting a room. He based his design for the

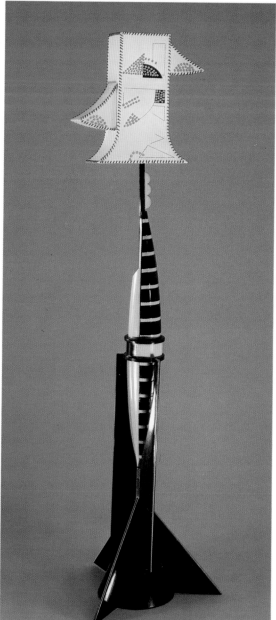

study-library room of the Ambassade Française at the 1925 Exposition around a central cupola, with sliding fan partitions to screen off light. His Maison de Verre of 1928-31, with its entire façade and many of its interior walls made of glass, is a brilliant exercise in filtering the maximum amount of daylight through to an interior without sacrificing a sense of the solidity of the structure and of an enclosed space.

His early lamps were decorative Cubist designs, typified by his standard lamp *'La Religieuse'*, with its conical tapering base and shade made up of triangular sections of alabaster set against one another in an irregular composition. In the early 1920s these designs were adapted to table lamps, wall sconces and ceiling lights. Chareau cleverly contrasted their sharp angles with the diffused glow that filtered from the alabaster slices. He recognized the value of light in softening the rather abrupt planes and forms of Modernist interiors, and favoured alabaster for its extreme translucence. He also used light fixtures to provide decorative interest and to unify large rooms, sometimes creating irregular patterns by scattering numerous small light fixtures across walls and ceilings. The device of using lighting to accentuate architectural features in an interior became very popular with modernistic designers.

Eileen Gray's early lighting designs were very strong and sculptural in conception, and so unusual that they outraged the critics when they were first exhibited. She was concerned with controling the flow of light as well as creating objects that were bold and interesting additions to a room. One ceiling lamp of hers was made up of a metal cylinder fitted at one end with an ostrich egg and pierced irregularly to emit a discreet, softened light. Quite dif-

Above left: Pair of table lamps, 1923, by Waldemar Raemisch; his work combined modernistic and primitive forms.

Above: Pair of lamps in frosted glass and chrome, c. 1928, by Jean Perzel, a technical innovator as well as a brilliant designer.

Left: Eileen Gray's standard lamp with lacquered support and painted parchment shade, 1923.

ferent again, and more modernistic in its stylish functionality, simple lines and conical parchment shade, is a floor lamp designed for the Salon des Artistes Décorateurs of 1923. Her parchment lampshades with appliquéd geometrical designs were perhaps the origin of the fashion that appeared much later in the 1930s for applying painted jazz motifs to parchment shades.

Many of the lamps designed by the more avant-garde artists were conceived as Cubist-type sculptures. Most of Eileen Gray's early lamps incorporate a Cubist treatment of forms and motifs. Jean Goulden created enameled table lamps and night lights which, like his clocks, were built up of juxtaposed planes, shapes and colors. The light source was embedded in the stand and treated as another decorative element in the design, set against the enamel and metal. Jean Lambert-Rucki sculpted elaborate bases for lamps in a style inspired by Cubism and African tribal art. These were usually crowned with a simple parchment shade. For the Deutsche Werkbund the painter and sculptor Waldemar Raemisch designed figural bronze table lamps in an individual style, a cross between modernistic machined and primitive forms.

Under the influence of Modernism, lighting became more functional and the pairing of metal and glass, so beloved of modernistic designers, began to predominate. With the general fashion for clean, bare and well-lit interiors, lighting was stripped of its silk shades, its thick moldings, its dim diffused quality, and became the focus of a search for clarity and maximum efficiency. Attention turned to the light source as prime element in the design, and lamps ceased to masquerade apologetically as *objets d'art*. Improvements in the manufacture of glass made it possible to cast glass in finer sections and therefore to produce a stronger light source. Globes or simple shapes

in frosted glass that radiated an even light became fashionable. These forms were carefully constructed and joined with tiny metal armatures, so that the seams were virtually invisible. A simple chromed metal stand, cylindrical or spherical, and wide conical shade either in parchment, frosted glass or similar translucent material was also popular. Lights were frequently set into walls and ceilings, disposing of the need for fixtures and sconces. But the decorative potential of lighting was never quite forgotten. René Herbst used lighting in a particularly sensitive way; his lighting designs were always delicate, stylish and unusual, giving a flourish to his over-orderly and even characterless interiors.

The Bauhaus artist Marianne Brandt turned from metalwork to lighting and devised functional lighting fixtures including the famous Kandem bedside light with push-button switch and adjustable reflector, which became a prototype for bedside lamps worldwide.

Jean Perzel was the master of modernistic lighting, a brilliant technician as well as an imaginative designer. He was a Czech who first came to Paris in 1910 to develop the technique of glass window decoration. From 1923 onward he specialized in lighting. His early experiments display an interest in improving the quality and distribution of light that was to dominate his career. He was fascinated by electricity and was concerned to present light in the best possible form, both from an aesthetic and a functional point of view. He investigated the psychological effect of good and bad lighting in an interior, recognizing that the brilliantly lit Modernist interior was rather too functional for comfort and ease. At first he used colorless glass in his designs, sandblasted and enameled to a restful degree of opacity so that the light filtered through evenly and was bright, but not too bright. Equally he sought to give rational form to the lighting device. His early designs did not eliminate the points of light formed by the bulb, and this led him to create overlapping geometrical shapes: disks, cylinders or a build-up of semi-cylinders, always devoid of ornament. Mounts were always minimal but by the early 1930s they were sometimes completely invisible, and fittings were reduced to simple geometrical shapes resembling sculptured light. His glass was mainly colorless; sometimes he added pinkish tints that cast a flattering glow, or hints of color to harmonize with a decor. Perzel held that lighting should not reduce an interior to an evenly illuminated box, but should take into account the play of shadows and reflected light. His polished metal shades and fitments were intended to reflect light.

Like Perzel, Boris Lacroix contributed intelligent designs to the field of lighting. He emphasized the role of metal, often using polished steel and nickel surfaces as light reflectors. His forms were simple and geometrical. Georges Lechevallier-Chevignard created stark machined forms from flat planes of metal, exposing the rivets and leaving the metal unpolished to create surface interest.

Equally bold in their way were the designs of the Adnet brothers, who were strongly influenced by Le Corbusier and were responsible for introducing the Modernist philosophy of truth to materials and simplicity of design to the field of lighting. They designed fixtures that flaunted bare bulbs, and exhibited a spectacular range of zigzagged tubular glass lights at the 1925 Exposition.

The Maison Desny was established around 1927, providing a complete range of furnishings in a smart, Cubist-inspired, geometrical style. Their lighting designs, illuminated sculptures in polished chrome and opaque glass, were clever and sophisticated constructions. Smart inexpensive fixtures in up-to-the-minute geometrical designs, often made of the early mottled plastic, were common in the late 1920s and 1930s.

In Britain lighting was used in hotels, restaurants, night clubs and cinemas to create dramatic Hollywood-style effects. The results range from merely gimmicky to strong and spectacular. Designers dreamt up multi-bulb

Left: Chromed metal and glass table lamp, late 1920s, by Maison Desny.

fixtures, starburst designs and illuminated panels. Upwardly directed lighting combined with decorative molding on a ceiling created a dramatic effect suitable for important entranceways; the best extant example of this can be seen in the foyer of the *Daily Express* building in London.

Below: Entrance to the Strand Palace Hotel, London, 1930s.

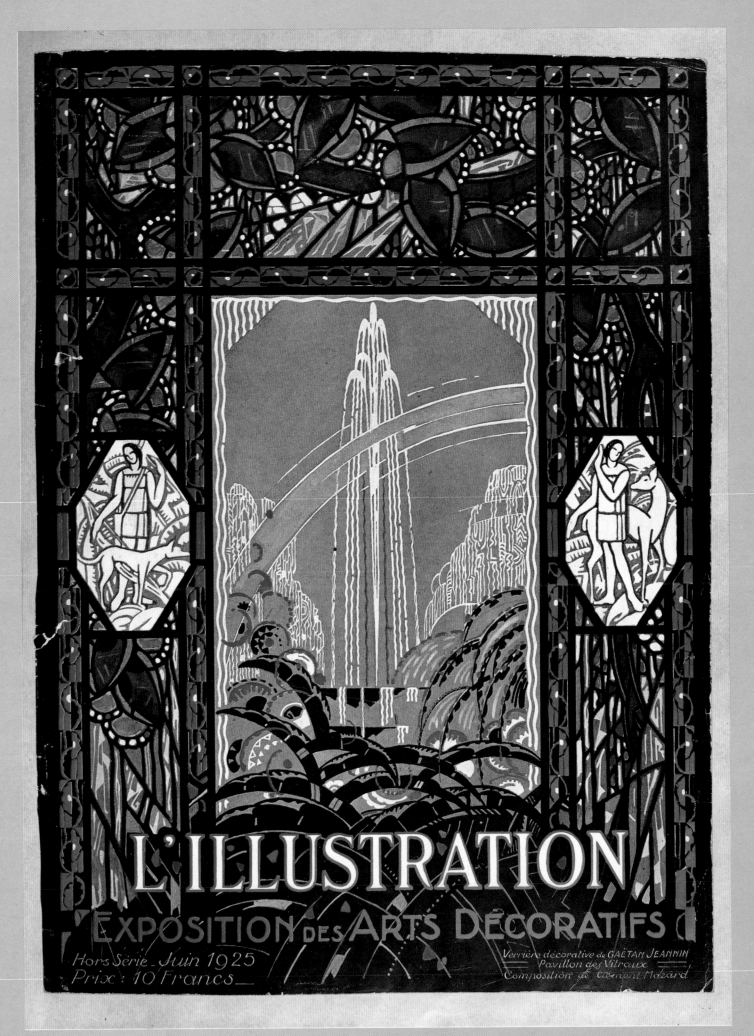

L'ILLUSTRATION

EXPOSITION DES ARTS DÉCORATIFS

Hors Série - Juin 1925
Prix : 10 Francs

Verrière décorative de GAËTAN JEANNIN
Pavillon des Vitraux
Composition de Clément Mazard

6
GLASS

From René Lalique, who developed techniques of mass-producing high quality glassware, to Maurice Marinot, who revised methods of handworking glass, the Art Deco period is characterized by a great variety of treatments and decorative effects in glass design. Glassworkers gained a degree of technical mastery of the material that gave them a new freedom in design and allowed them to break completely with past styles. In the latter half of the period, glass attained a status it had never enjoyed before, and its uses and applications multiplied.

The story of the modernization of glass really begins with the Art Nouveau *maîtres verriers* – Emile Gallé, Eugène Rousseau and Dammouse – who revived craftsmanlike techniques and pioneered new ones. The best of the glassworkers who succeeded them continued to focus on materials and methods of production as a means of creating a strong modern style of glassware.

Pâte-de-verre had been popular with Art Nouveau glassworkers, and came back into vogue during the 1920s and 1930s. It is made by mixing finely ground glass with a fluxing agent. The resultant paste is colored by adding metallic oxides or granules of colored glass, molded or modeled into the desired form, and then fired at a high temperature. The colors fuse into one another, and the glass takes on a jewel-like translucent quality with a slightly waxy surface rather like soapstone. *Pâte-de-verre's* brilliant color effects distinguish it from other glass of the interwar period, much of which was either monochrome or clear.

François-Emile Décorchemont and Joseph-Gabriel Argy-Rousseau were the two great Art Deco *pâte-de-verre* artists. Décorchemont's work of the first decade of the century was in the Art Nouveau style, highly decorative and modeled in opaque, brittle glass that closely resembled enamel, but around 1910 he had begun to concentrate on creating larger forms. Bold, thick-walled vessels, streaked and swirled with color to evoke the mottled effect of antique glass, marble or other hardstones are characteristic of this later style. Color continued to be an important element in Décorchemont's work and he developed a range of brilliant and unusual hues, including a semi-translucent golden brown resembling tortoiseshell. The shapes of his vessels became more geometrical and handles were often emphasized, sometimes designed in the form of stylized animals, while the vessels themselves were decorated with flowers and fruit. In the late 1920s forms were simplified still further and became more angular, often molded in imitation of carved stone and still in the jewel-like colors of his earlier work. By the mid-1930s he had shifted his interest to the creation of large panels in *pâte-de-verre*, a richer, more opaque alternative to leaded glass.

Argy-Rousseau also made *pâte-de-verre* his speciality and set up a company to manufacture his extensive range of decorative objects, each item individually colored and finished. Much of his work was lightweight and opaque, decorated with flowers and animals and often displaying the lingering influence of Art Nouveau glassware. But he is better known for his designs in *pâte-de-cristal* (the addition of lead enriched and clarified the colors) which were molded with neoclassical motifs. He developed a more angular geometrical style in the late 1920s and 1930s, creating chunky vases and bowls that were swirled or streaked with translucent color.

Another group of glassworkers of this period were exploring the rich color effects and clarity of definition of enameled glass. Marcel Goupy was an important exponent of this technique, and his assistant Auguste-Claude Heiligenstein became a notable enamelist in his own right. The crisp quality of enamel was particularly suited to Art Deco stylizations. Goupy specialized in a high Deco repertoire of birds, flowers, animals and figurative designs – female nudes and mythological figures – which he painted onto the surfaces of his glass vessels in brightly colored enamels. He produced mostly decorative ware, although he did design some cleverly co-ordinated tableware in glass and ceramic.

Below: *Pâte-de-verre* vase by Gabriel Argy-Rousseau.

The Daum company of Nancy made its name at the end of the nineteenth century with a successful range of Art Nouveau glassware in the style of Emile Gallé. In 1919 the company re-opened, producing a range of simple geometrical vessels that were internally colored with swirls of metal oxides, or overlays of gold, silver or platinum foils which broke up into a multitude of tiny specks. Sometimes this glass was blown into iron armatures by Edgar Brandt, or used to make shades for his lampstands. No doubt Daum was influenced by the thick-walled, heavily textured style of Maurice Marinot's work when, in the mid-1920s, they developed a style characterized by deeply etched angular designs on a simple, chunky, glass form and typically colored in greens, blues and oranges. Standard Deco motifs of geometricized fruit, flowers and abstract patterns were etched away in relief with acid, so that the design stood out smooth-surfaced against a rough-textured background.

Schneider, among other companies, took to etching their vessels and produced a range of cheerful and elegant colored glass that was lightly patterned in Deco-style geometrical designs. They also produced a range of glassware in mottled marblized colors. Jean Luce achieved similar contrasts of rough and smooth by sand-blasting geometrical decorations onto plain forms, and sometimes applied mirrored or gilded finishes in abstract geometrical patterns.

The highly versatile and talented René Lalique abandoned his career as a successful Art Nouveau jeweler to become a brilliant *maître verrier* working in the high Art Deco style. He first used glass in his jewelry designs and began making glass experimentally as early as 1890. The year 1908 really marks his switch to glasswork, when he was commissioned by the *parfumiers* Coty to design scent bottles and packaging. From that time on Lalique concentrated increasingly on glass design, taking over first a glassworks and then later a larger workshop, where he could apply industrial techniques of production and therefore mass produce his wares and reduce costs. The new medium absorbed him totally and by around 1915 he had almost ceased designing jewelry.

Lalique tended to work in *demi-cristal*, glass with a 50 percent lead content. The quality both of design and production was consistently high, so much so that many of his pieces seem too exquisite to be made of mere glass. He was a technical wizard, endlessly experimenting with different methods of achieving contrasting finishes: frosting with acids; enameling and staining to accent relief molding; exposing glass to a mixture of gases to produce an antiquated patina; buffing the glass to polish it. By sandwiching opaque glass between

layers of colorless glass, he achieved wonderful opalescent effects that softened the *demi-cristal* and gave it an unearthly, lunar quality. His early designs were influenced by Art Nouveau but by around 1913 he had developed a style that was rational and harmonious; forms were simple, decorated in molded relief with female nudes, birds, fish, fruit, flowers and other motifs drawn from nature. Most of his output was in this graceful classical style, but he also designed some streamlined modernistic pieces in the late 1920s, including a series of

Above: Victoire, molded glass car mascot, 1929, by René Lalique, an example of his streamlined modernistic style.

Below: François-Emile Décorchemont's *pâte-de-verre* bowl, 1920s.

Right: Mottled glass vase enameled with classical figures, c. 1925, by Marcel Goupy.

Below: Acid-etched blue glass vase, 1930s, by the Daum company.

car mascots, and some of his naturalistic forms were rendered in a near-abstract fashion. Usually the glass was blown mechanically or by mouth into prepared molds, or cast in a stamping press. From the mid-1920s Lalique made a few unique pieces using the *cire perdue* method adapted from bronze casting; a model carved in wax was covered in clay, the wax was melted out and replaced with molten glass. These were in a different category from his commercial output and were subtly textured, often even marked with his own fingerprints.

By the end of his career Lalique had virtually exhausted the applications of glass, and his repertoire included sculpture and ornamental pieces, tableware, vases, toiletry items, jewelry, clock cases, light fixtures, mirrors, tables, fountains and architectural fittings. The last included panels for London's Claridge's Hotel and, probably his most spectacular architectural assignment, the first-class dining room for the liner *Normandie*, with vast chandeliers and illuminated light panels, glass panels covering the walls and an illuminated coffered ceiling. His numerous lighting designs reflect his sensitivity to the play of light on glass, and particularly on etched and relief surfaces. Lalique exhibited widely at the 1925 Exposition, to great critical acclaim. His style was enormously popular, particularly during the 1920s and

Below: René Lalique's grasshopper vase, an early design from c. 1920.

1930s, and was much imitated, both in France and abroad.

While Lalique used industrial methods to mass produce his work, Maurice Marinot emphasized the craft aspect of glasswork and each of his pieces was handworked and unique. Marinot was largely responsible for the change in direction that glass design took during this period. The decorative possibilities, the techniques, the materials, the forms, all were entirely rethought and the results were utterly new. He combined craftsmanlike techniques with an accumulated knowledge of the properties of glass. His output was relatively small and each piece was laboriously and painstakingly crafted.

Marinot began his career as a painter and was associated with the Fauves school, but a visit to the glassworks of some friends inspired him to train as a glassworker and he began gradually to make experiments of his own. By 1913 he was concentrating almost exclusively on glass design. His first essays consisted of figurative decoration, rather painterly in style, which he applied in bright enamels. His interest in developing new techniques led him to experiment with ways of creating enamels that were translucent rather than opaque, and methods of layering the enamel so that it integrated with the glass. In the early 1920s he abandoned

Right: Carved and chiseled glass vase, late 1920s, by Aristide Colotte, who specialized in sculptural effects.

Far right: Carved and frosted glass vase by Aristide Colotte.

Below: This glass vase with three girls was designed by Vicke Lindstrand for Orrefors.

superficially applied decoration altogether and began to blow his own glass vessels and work the mass of the glass into sculptural forms while it was still hot, exploiting qualities inherent in the material and faults in composition to create abstract decorative effects. He would allow air bubbles to form and trap them between layers of clear glass; apply internal whirls and streaks of color; tease out impurities in the glass; or apply chemicals for crackled effects. Generally a smooth outer surface pro-

vided contrast to the internal texture. He also produced more dynamic sculptural effects by repeated bathing in hydrofluoric acid, which etched away at thick glass vessels in crude geometrical relief; many of these pieces resemble blocks of melted ice. Later still he worked vessels at the furnace, modeling and carving directly into the glass or building up a piece with numerous applications of molten glass, again for massive sculptural effects. Sometimes he applied primitive mask designs in molten glass. His vessels are thick-walled and massive and bottles are crowned with tiny spherical stoppers. Basic forms are simple ovoid, cylindrical and spherical gourd shapes. Marinot went on working in glass until the late 1930s. His work found recognition early on and most of his pieces were quickly bought up by museums. He had many imitators, and exercised a considerable influence on glass design of the interwar years in France and elsewhere in Europe, liberating it from conventional treatments. Henri Navarre was his greatest follower, and continued to develop Marinot's techniques of internal decoration (with powdered oxides, streaks and bubbles) and of working at the kiln, though in a style more elaborate than Marinot's and often in crystal rather than glass.

Aristide Colotte also favored largescale sculptural effects, but his method was to carve and chisel at the glass. In his mature phase he executed some extremely forceful, purely abstract pieces, but he never entirely abandoned figurative and animal themes. Sometimes he carved glass figures at the wheel and etched away at blocks of raw glass or crystal, creating highly polished and rough finishes that generate an interesting play of light.

In the wake of Lalique's success, derivative molded glass was produced all over Europe, particularly in Italy, England and in France itself. There was also, however, much innovation in modern glass design throughout

Left: Louis Barillet's stained glass window wall in the Bally shoe store in Paris. The architect responsible for the design of the new shoe store was Robert Mallet-Stevens, who collaborated with Barillet on a number of projects.

Europe. A number of designers attached to the Wiener Werkstätte produced modern glassware; Hoffmann, Moser and Dagobert Peche were the most notable. In Denmark, Finland and the Netherlands there were companies producing everyday and art glass in the modern idiom, and they often drew their inspiration from the immense creative output of the French glassworkers.

Glassworkers in Sweden earned a high reputation in this period, particularly those of the Orrefors factory, who developed a style similar in spirit to but not derivative of French design. During World War I a campaign had been launched by the Swedish Society of Industrial Design based on the ideas of Hermann Muthesius, with the aim of encouraging the application of good design to industry. The Orrefors company was one of the first to take advantage of this new union of art with industry. Simon Gate and Edward Hald were employed to initiate the scheme. Gate chose to investigate the cameo technique (a design was acid-etched on to a vessel, fused at the furnace and then sandwiched in clear glass and polished), which was characteristic of Art Nouveau and Emile Gallé's work, out of which he developed the Graal technique (layers of glass were etched or carved with relief decoration and these images were fused in the furnace). Hald on the other hand, who had studied under Matisse in Paris, introduced a more modernistic element into the firm's design. Both Gate and Hald executed a good deal of mainly figurative wheel-engraved decoration. In the late 1920s they were joined by Edvin Ohrström and Vicke Lindstrand, who contributed a forceful Modernist

element to the Orrefors output. Ohrström developed a variation of the Graal technique, which involved trapping patterns of air bubbles in a case of clear glass and which he called the Ariel technique. The Orrefors exhibits at the 1925 Exposition received great acclaim and influenced designers throughout Europe.

Czechoslovakia had long been renowned for its glassware and produced a range of bold

Below: Glass dressing table and stool, 1933, by Oliver Hill for Pilkington Glass.

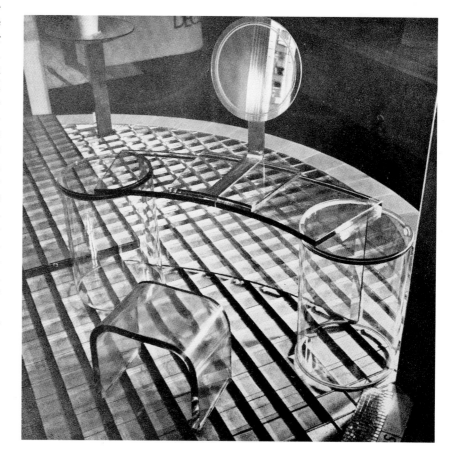

Right: Glass vase, wheel-cut with vertical and horizontal grooves, 1937, by Keith Murray for Stevens and Williams.

Cubist-inspired wares. Equally sophisticated Deco glassware was coming out of Germany and Belgium. In Britain, however, traditional glass designs predominated and the output of the 1920s and 1930s was notably uninspired and lacking in quality. In general cheap, well-designed glassware was imported from abroad. Some decorative glass was produced in imitation of French and Swedish styles, but the best work in the Modernist idiom was done by the New Zealander Keith Murray, who was also an architect and a designer of silver and ceramics. His interest in designing glass stemmed from a deep admiration for eighteenth-century English glass and was further stimulated by his visit to the 1925 Exposition, where he saw the Swedish, and particularly the Orrefors exhibit, and also admired the Finnish and Czechoslovakian glass. He began designing glassware in 1931 for Stevens and Williams of Brierley Hill, Staffordshire. For Murray form was supremely important –

Right: René Lalique: *Trépied Sirène* bowl, made of opalescent glass with molded design and raised on three low feet.

teriors such as theatre foyers and hotels. Mirror too became a fashionable material and enjoyed the same variety of applications; furniture, walls, floors, even clocks and boxes were mirrored.

Verre églomisé panels (glass painted and highlighted in gold and silver leaf on the reverse) were popular as largescale lavish and decorative murals. The most famous was the series of panels designed by Jean Dupas for the French ocean liner *Normandie*, depicting the history of navigation.

A few artists devoted themselves to modernizing techniques of staining glass and other aspects of the craft. Jacques Gruber designed figurative compositions in an angular 1920s style, while Louis Barillet worked in a strictly geometrical idiom and a restricted range of colors, mainly tones of gray, white and black. He worked frequently with Mallet-Stevens and designed leaded glass friezes for his Pavillon de Tourisme at the 1925 Exposition.

Left: Hand-blown flask and stopper, 1929, by Maurice Marinot.

Below: Maurice Marinot's engraved, stoppered bottle with interior decoration; a more tactile, eye-catching design than the classic example above.

decoration was often minimal, consisting simply of a little machined fluting, and colors were restrained, although he did also design more decorative pieces, some with jazzy enameled motifs, others with engraved Swedish-style designs.

In Italy Venini revived the stultified glass industry of Venice, which had been endlessly repeating the designs of its sixteenth-century heyday, with smart, scarcely ornamented pieces and experiments with color and texture. A visit to the 1925 Exposition generated a number of interesting interpretations of the Art Deco theme by various Italian glassworkers.

The importance and range of uses of glass increased throughout the 1920s, and by the end of the decade it enjoyed the status of 'material of the moment', alongside aluminum, steel and concrete. Glass became associated with light, cleanliness, purity and hygiene: all the qualities of modern living. The Modernists (particularly the Bauhaus artists) did much to exalt glass and to expand its applications and uses, most notably in the field of architecture. In 1920 Mies Van der Rohe designed a skyscraper entirely clad in glass. Architects such as Chareau and Mallet-Stevens took up the glass theme and made innovative use of it in their own designs. The façade of Chareau's Maison de Verre of 1928-31 was made entirely of glass bricks and panels, and most of the internal partitions were glass too. Glass, as well as being practical and hygenic was chic – hard, glossy and smooth – and as such was appealing as a furnishing material. Coffered glass ceilings, paneled glass walls and glass tiles on the floor were the height of chic and sophistication in the late 1920s and early 1930s, especially if illuminated. Illuminated wall paneling was particularly suited to spectacular and grand in-

7
SILVER

Silver is not a metal usually associated with innovative or avant-garde design. Because of its value it has always been reserved for luxury objects, and designs for silverware have tended to be of the most conservative and traditional type. This was particularly true of the early twentieth century, when Art Deco was beginning to permeate the decorative arts. It was chiefly thanks to the brilliant technical and design skills of Jean Puiforcat that silverware made so successful a transition from tradition to modernity. Not only was he the best silversmith of the period, he also ranked among the best of all Art Deco designers. Along with a handful of other silversmiths he showed that designs for silverware could be brought up to date in an elegant and dignified fashion. In their wake the manufacturers of silverware began tentatively to contribute modern designs, and silverware slowly followed the evolution of the other decorative arts.

Like gold, silver is a soft and malleable metal and can be worked in a variety of ways. Forms can be rendered either by cutting, casting or hammering. Most of the best Deco silversmiths made use of the new techniques of stamping, spinning and casting silver but finished the pieces by hand. The laborious technique of hammering the metal was not used for com-

mercial production. After the 1929 Wall Street crash, the demand for silverware virtually ceased and plated metals became increasingly common. Some firms would offer versions of the same design in both solid and plated silver.

Puiforcat's family were goldsmiths and he began his career by serving as an apprentice in his father's firm, before going on to study sculpture for a time. He exhibited his first designs at the Salon d'Automne of 1921. By the following year the Musée des Arts Décoratifs had bought one of his pieces, and his genius was confirmed.

From the first Puiforcat's designs were innovative. He eschewed surface ornament altogether and concentrated on simplifying form to its most functional and minimal. The task he set himself was not by any means a simple one, for the silver could easily appear dull and lifeless without its habitual surface embellishments. Only by studying the properties and qualities of the metal in relation to design was he able to create pieces that were restrained and elegant, and yet at the same time played on the rich tonal effects of the metal. His work is absolutely unembellished; surfaces are as smooth and shiny as satin and bear none of the hammer marks of traditional handmade silverware. These smooth planes are built up into

Below: Silver and ivory tea-service, 1920s, by Jean Puiforcat, one of the foremost Deco designers.

Left: Jean Puiforcat's silver flatware service, 1920s.

Below: Jean Puiforcat's silver and onyx clock, c. 1932, illustrates his interest in geometrical harmony.

beautifully proportioned forms. A clever device he used to enliven his designs was to facet a piece almost imperceptibly, so that reflected light was thrown off at different angles. Like the best glassworkers, he understood the importance of manipulating the play of light on surfaces. He also discovered that certain rare woods or semi-precious stones, incorporated as handles and finials, successfully complemented a simple form and added to the play of reflections and tones, as well as emphasizing textural contrasts.

Platonic ideals of simplicity and harmony govern the design of Puiforcat's pieces. All his forms are derived from basic geometrical shapes and relate to each other according to arithmetical proportions. Beyond being functional, a piece had to be as graceful as he was able to make it. His perfectly executed designs on paper bear witness to a meticulous and highly organized method of design, based on three fundamental shapes; the sphere, cone and cylinder. His output included many coffee and tea services, liturgical pieces, flatware and candlesticks, table lamps, even chess sets in silver, ivory and ebony – all supremely elegant pieces, often embellished with lapis-lazuli, crystal, tinted glass, ebony or ivory. His tableware is equally understated and plain, at most ornamented with a little discreet fluting or banding.

Puiforcat was a founder member of the Union des Artistes Modernes, which was formed in 1930. Like other members of the UAM, he worked in a pared-down style that

aimed to unify design and function, but he did not embrace Modernist ideals of mass production. He believed in principle in the dissemination of good design through industry, but felt that he himself could not mass produce his own designs without loss of quality.

Another silversmith responsible for the rejuventation of silver design was Jean Tétard. His firm, Tétard *frères*, was one of the few that chose not to cling to tradition but to introduce a

bold modern style for functional tableware. His work displays great technical virtuosity; forms are complex but also largely undecorated, generally with handles carved in rich rare woods.

A number of noted Art Deco designers created modernistic silverware for the Parisian firm Christofle, which was one of the most advanced of the large firms selling metalwork. They included Gio Ponti, the pewtersmith

Left: Silver vegetable dish by the Danish silversmith Georg Jensen, an example of his plainer more modernistic style.

Maurice Daurat, André Groult, Paul Follot and Christian Fjerdlingstad. Christofle purchased most of the patents for the electroplating system of silver plating which was developed in the nineteenth century, and during the Art Deco period produced a good deal of electroplated tableware. One of the few large firms producing silverware in the Art Deco style, they were very successul and marketed abroad in London, Vienna, and in America. Gio Ponti's designs for silver are characteristically elegant, with sleek and tapering forms, while the Dane Christian Fjerdlingstad worked in an elegant minimalist style.

Süe et Mare's great dominion extended over silverware too, and Louis Süe designed both for his own Compagnie des Arts Français and for Christofle. His pieces are elegantly shaped, based on traditional forms, and faceted in the Cubist manner. Süe et Mare also designed some silverware in their characteristically elaborate decorative manner.

The jeweler Jean Desprès created very plain objects in silver that were often rather angular and exaggeratedly Cubist in treatment. His surfaces are unornamented but hammered to a rough texture, to create a lively play of light and tone, rather than smooth and shiny. He made no attempt to disguise bolts and rivets but incorporated them into his designs as 'decoration'. Shapes were deliberately fashioned to resemble machine parts. Another jeweler and independent craftsman, Gérard Sandoz, produced a number of refined and unusual silver objects which he embellished with sumptuous materials like shagreen, lizard skin and ivory. He too hammered the metal to create a textured finish and flaunted bolts and rivets. Unlike Puiforcat's pieces, these often aggressively moder-

nistic designs can now seem rather clumsy and dated.

The Parisian firm Desny produced more sophisticated, modernistic silverware for a fashionable clientele – their sleek conical cocktail sets were particularly popular. Many of their pieces were silver-plated and therefore not prohibitive in price.

Below: Box in silver and ivory by Charles Boyton, c. 1930.

During this period much ingenuity was employed in the design of clocks. Now that clocks could be run by electricity they did not need to be so large and cumbersome, nor did they need to be strategically placed for easy winding. Clock design therefore offered a relatively unconstrained opportunity for the artist to display his creative and innovative talents. Art Deco clocks range in style from tiny and jewel-like, through floral and fussy, to rigorous and modernistic examples. Designs are often quirky or eccentric but the best are also exciting and unusual. One of the most interesting clocks of the period is a minimalist arrangement of numerals, hands and base in silver designed by Puiforcat. Melik Minassiantz invented a clock that had no hands, but indicated the time by a system of balls rotating in circular grooves. Albert Cheuret is best known for his lighting devices, but he also designed a number of clocks in silvered bronze, most notable of which is his clock styled in the Egyptian mode with Egyptian numerals and Egyptian headdress surround.

At the same time there was quite a vogue for rather gimmicky compact silver tea services, the various elements designed to fit together to make up an amusing and unusual display, although the individual pieces, being so rigidly geometrical, were not always terribly functional. Boris Lacroix, Desny, Gérard Sandoz and Charles Boyton all designed variations on this compact cubic theme, often with matching trays.

In England a design for a teapot compacted into a cube shape was introduced in the early 1920s. By the late 1920s and 1930s it was available both in ceramic and silver and had become widely popular, despite the fact that the spouts were ineffective and the handles could not be properly grasped. Much of the modern silverware in Britain was in this very angular style, reflecting the quest for novelty and modernity.

The Bauhaus artist Marianne Brandt was a metalworker before she turned to lighting design. In the 1920s she designed some fine silver pieces, many of them based on an interesting play of curves. These were far more elegant and less austere than the majority of silver and metalware designs coming out of the Bauhaus at this time.

Georg Jensen was a Danish silversmith whose firm, based in Copenhagen, produced a

wide range of goods in silver. His firm sold silverware in a variety of styles, including an elaborate high Deco characterized by its decorative scrolls, flowers and leaves, as well as a more modernistic, plain style. Jensen himself had a powerful influence on silver design of the period. He was notable for making many of his pieces accessible to the growing middle classes by producing relatively inexpensive silverware. He had a number of designers working for him, but was a formidable designer himself. He developed a style in the 1920s that was elegant and modernistic but not utterly plain, for he frequently used little silver beads as a decorative device. Sometimes he set his pieces with semi-precious stones.

The architect Harald Nielsen also worked for Jensen, contributing a functionalist style that was influenced by the Bauhaus. He was famous for his 'pyramid' cutlery design.

Jensen's fame spread as he began to open branches around Europe – first in Berlin in 1908, then in Paris in 1919, in London in 1920 and a little later in New York and Stockholm.

The development of silver design in England in the 1920s was held back by the dominance of the Arts and Crafts style. Charles Boyton was one of the few who broke away from the Arts and Crafts manner. He worked in a strong angular style and favored compact shapes and the use of fine woods and ivory for handles and finials. Other silversmiths incorporated stylized floral and geometrical motifs in the Parisian manner. H G Murphy created a series of boxes with plain bodies and elaborate finials, often incorporating exotic materials like coral and ivory.

JEWELRY

Opposite: Van Cleef and Arpels's 'mystery' clock – a jade bear on a base of black onyx supporting a crystal disk set with rose-cut diamonds, 1930s.

rt Deco craftsmen broke with traditional styles of jewelry, as well as conventions as to how it should be worn, but they owed much to Art Nouveau jewelers who had already wrought considerable changes; their use of non-precious and semi-precious materials in conjunction with precious stones and metals was particularly inspiring to the jewelers of the interwar period, setting a high standard of inventiveness and creativity which was emulated by their successors. Tortoiseshell, ivory, mother-of-pearl, enamel, lacqueur and glass were all materials introduced by Art Nouveau and exploited by Art Deco jewelers.

Although there were a few adherents of the Deco style in jewelry outside France, more so after the 1925 Exposition, Paris remained the center of the great surge of creativity in jewelry design. Long-established firms such as Mauboussin, Cartier and Boucheron still dominated the jewelry scene and successfully adapted to the Deco style; Louis Cartier, Raymond Templier, Jean Fouquet and Gérard Sandoz were all grandsons of the men who had founded their respective firms. These firms used their own in-house designers as well as buying or commissioning designs from independent artists.

The vibrant colors that began to dominate the decorative arts before World War I sent jewelry designers in search of new materials to add to those introduced by the Art Nouveau jewelers. Striking contrasts were created, with diamonds and other precious stones and metals set against the smooth surfaces and uniform color of hardstones such as coral, jade, black and white onyx, lapis lazuli, turquoise, amber and malachite. Mauboussin were particularly renowned for their colorful jewelry.

Diamonds never really go out of fashion but they were given a fresh lease of life during this period, thanks to a Dutch diamond-cutting firm outside Paris which devised new ways of faceting stones. Their *baguette* cut – the diamond cut into a thin faceted rectangular form – set against diamonds or gemstones of other cuts, created an almost Cubist juxtaposition of planes and forms, and luminous effects of refracted light. The *baguette* cut was a notable feature of jewelry design from the early 1920s. Diamonds were traditionally the focal point of a piece of jewelry but were not always so prominently displayed in this period. They were often used to highlight the lines of a piece, or juxtaposed with other gemstones and hardstones to create interesting color combinations.

The display of technical virtuosity was an important feature of jewelry design of the period. Jewelers took pride in creating invisible settings and flexible structures for stones; bracelets and necklaces resembled ribbons of pure color. Platinum was a recent discovery and became popular. It was easy to work but immensely strong, enabling jewelers to set stones almost invisibly in open-claw settings, rather than the traditional metal cup. The light platinum mounts allowed light to pass through transparent stones, thus showing them to far better advantage than previously. Pearls were widely used, chiefly because they were now available in large numbers through the new method of culturing devised by the Japanese Mikimoto. Rock crystal was admired for its limpid quality, as well as for its velvety matt surface when frosted, and was used a good deal in composite jewelry designs.

Jewelry design showed a marked tendency to simplification and stylization, and motifs

Below: Earrings in gold, ivory and enamel, rings in yellow and white gold, coral, carnelian and onyx, all c. 1925, by Raymond Templier.

Below right: Boucheron's drop earrings in jade, onyx and diamonds, 1920s.

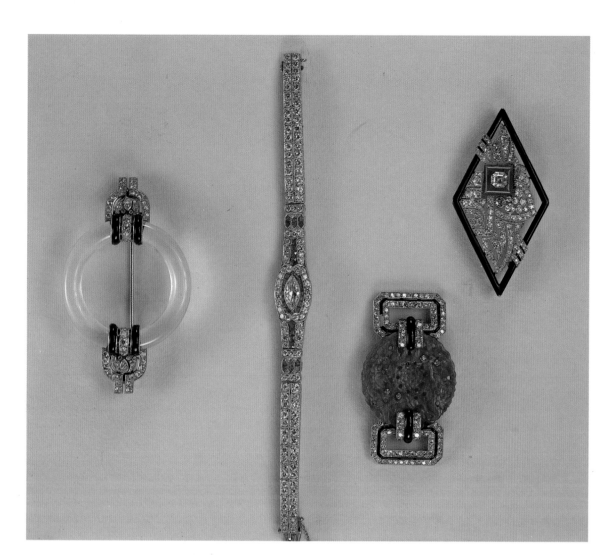

ranged from stylized figurative to geometric abstraction. Elaborate multicolored clusters of gemstones, skilfully worked into leaf, fruit or flower shapes to form brooches, buckles, rings and pendants, were popular. The stylized flower basket, so typical of Art Deco design, was a motif common to jewelry too. Many designers drew on a knowledge of the foreign art forms that inspired Art Deco, in particular those of the Orient. The firms of Cartier and Lacloche specialized in Oriental-style accessories and jewelry. Materials such as jade, coral, lacquer and enamel were used for their color, and jade and coral were frequently carved with Chinese motifs. The Egyptian craze that followed the discovery of Tutankhamun's tomb in 1922 was reflected as much in jewelry design as in the other decorative arts, while the colonial exhibitions of 1922 and 1931 helped to initiate a vogue for carved African jewelry that reached its height in the 1930s.

The developments in women's fashion of the period had a pronounced effect on jewelry design. As the whole aspect of women's dress radically changed, so the type and look and placement of jewelry changed too. As women's fashions became plainer jewelry played an increasingly important role, often providing the only decorative element in a woman's dress. Long ropes of pearls or bead necklaces (of

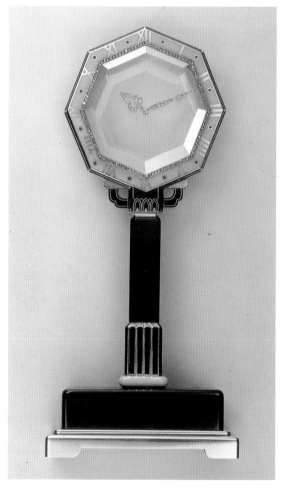

coral, lapis lazuli, jade, agate, mother-of-pearl), *sautoirs* and pendant necklaces were worn to the waist or even to the knees to accentuate the vertical lines of the new tubular dresses. These ropes were worn in a multitude of different ways: down the back or tossed over a shoulder, knotted and looped. With their heavy tassels and pendants they were designed to sway gently to the movement of the wearer; jewels perpetually in motion. Bracelets were flat, articulated bands, often worn two or more to one arm. When the full flapper style was in fashion, arms were bared and wide bangles known as slave bracelets were worn on the upper arm, as well as quantities of smaller bracelets and bangles. The brutally short hair cuts were softened and feminized with the addition of dangling pendant earrings, worn long to emphasize the length of the neck. Jeweled bandeaux worn about the head replaced the tiara for evening wear. By day cloche hats, pulled down over the eyes, were frequently decorated with jewels, buckles and particularly the little clips that became ubiquitous in the 1930s. These little clips were also worn on shoulders, sleeves, hips, belts, in the hair for evening, and in the hollow of the back when the back decolleté became fashionable. At first they were designed as fruit baskets, stylized flower bouquets, or more abstract scrolled composition. Larger brooches were often composed of rings of carved rock crystal, jade, onyx or coral surmounted with other stones. Rings were generally large and simple, often set with single stones.

The wristwatch became popular in the early Art Deco period, a fashion that was led by the tennis star Suzanne Lenglen. These were worn with silk or leather straps by day, while the evening version was a jeweled bracelet with a tiny, almost invisible face. In the latter half of the 1920s the pendant watch came into its own,

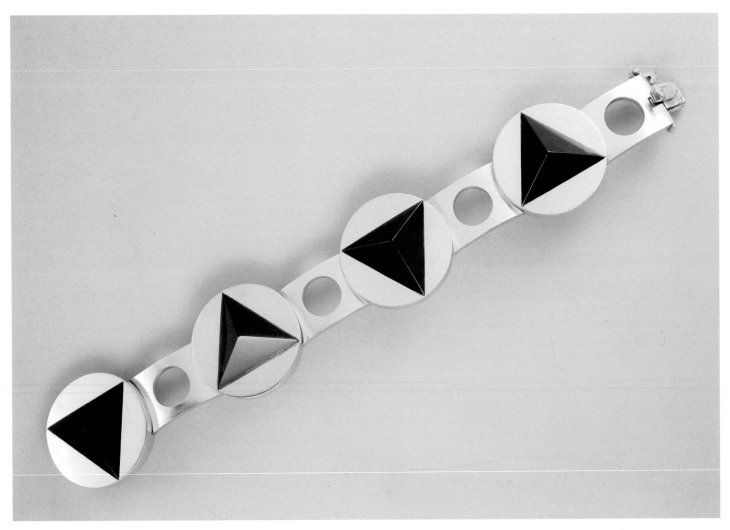

and was worn as a jewel with the watch face hidden from view. Watches and cufflinks decorated in simple colorful geometrical designs were the only jeweled objects worn by men.

Louis Cartier was responsible for guiding the Cartier firm into the new mode of design. From quite early on in his career he abandoned traditional design techniques and methods of setting jewels, and became one of the pioneering exponents of the multicolored mixing of precious and non-precious stones. He shared the prevalent Ballets Russes-inspired enthusiasm for the exotic, particularly Persian and Oriental style. Georges Fouquet worked in a less elaborate idiom, despite the fact that he had begun his career as an Art Nouveau jeweler. His designs were simple and dramatic, employing the full range of colorful hardstones.

René Lalique's jewelry design gave way to his interest in glass but he did continue to create some jewelry, mostly pendants of tinted and molded glass. These were hung on long, tasseled, silk cords or strings of glass beads, and decorated with typical motifs: insects, flowers, nymphs, leaves or animals. He also designed molded glass plaques to be set into metal frames for brooches, and flexible bracelets made of glass sections strung together on elastic cords. Other glassworkers, particularly the *pâte de verre* specialists, also designed glass jewelry.

A number of designers worked in a radical Modernist style that was clearly, if not directly, related to the stark functionalism of the Bauhaus. Gérard Sandoz, Jean Fouquet, Jean Desprès, Suzanne Belperron, Raymond Templier and Paul Brandt all contributed an abstract, machined aspect to jewelry designed in the 1920s and 1930s. In the world of high-class jewelry they formed an avant-garde, seeking to break completely with traditional ornamental styles and to create a new idiom for jewelry design, based on modern architectural and sculptural forms and inspired by the machine and the dynamics of speed. Much of their work also showed an awareness and appreciation of contemporary painting. The jumble of colors gave way to muted metallic tones highlighted with the addition of a single gem, or stark contrasts of black, red and white. Under their influence jewelry became angular and geometrical, bolder and less complex. They stressed the need for simplicity and the importance of being able to read a piece from a distance. More concerned with a high standard of design and innovative use of materials than with creating pieces of staggering expense, they began to blur the distinction between costume jewelry and *haute joaillerie*. Materials were chosen chiefly for their aesthetic and tactile qualities.

Most of this group were members of the Union des Artistes Modernes, of which Ray-

Above: Cartier's diamond, black onyx and emerald bangle, 1920s, with panther-head clasps.

mond Templier was a founding member. He developed a graceful modernistic style that was less harsh and aggressive than work by other artists. His simple geometrical patterns and juxtapositions of materials, particularly the varied tones of gold, platinum, and even stainless steel, were highly inventive. He often combined platinum and diamonds. Jean Fouquet, son of Georges, was a far more radical designer than his father. He too worked in a stark geometrical style, and such decoration as he used was engine-turned. He liked to contrast the tones of metals and juxtapose matt, highly polished and grooved surfaces with the contrasting textures of cut jewels or the carved hemisphere of a hardstone, usually in an assymetrical composition. His approach was sculptural and tactile, based on a play of relief against flat surfaces.

The best of Gérard Sandoz's work was confined to the latter half of the 1920s, and he gave up designing jewelry in 1931 to become a film director and painter. Even his early jewelry designs are absolutely stark and modernistic, inspired by Cubist forms and industrial parts. Metals are notched and incised, matt and polished, and generally set with a large single stone; cool metallic tones contrast with the relative warmth of labradorite, citrine or coral. Overlapping, assymetrical forms are characteristic of his style. He designed a range of lacquered cigarette cases, compacts and pocket

Right (clockwise from top left): Pair of clips, diamonds, onyx, white gold and platinum, c. 1925 by Paul Brandt; brooch, *pavé* diamonds, onyx and platinum, c. 1925 by Raymond Templier; brooch, rock crystal, onyx and white gold, c. 1930 by Paul Brandt; brooch, diamonds, onyx and white gold, c. 1925 by Mauboussin; all examples of the use of geometrical motifs.

Opposite: Necklace of silver, glass, imitation pearls and rhinestones, 1923, by Coco Chanel, who made costume jewelry fashionable.

Below: Chrome and bakelite necklaces, c. 1925, designed in a heavy primitive style.

Below right Mother-of-pearl, coral and diamond cigarette case, reminiscent in style of Oriental lacquerwork.

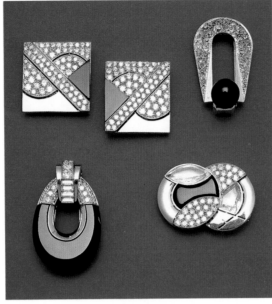

watches decorated with bold geometrical motifs in primary colors.

Jean Desprès began as early as 1912 to experiment with translating forms based on machine parts into jewelry design. He was trained as a silversmith and executed his own designs, working almost exclusively in metal, occasionally adding a little lacquer for contrast. His bracelets often have a textured hand-beaten surface. His work, made up of pure geometrical forms derived from industry, was highly sculptural, composed of spheres, cylinders and cubes.

The lacquer master and metalworker Jean Dunand designed some lacquered jewelry, as well as vanity and cigarette cases decorated with abstract geometrical patterns on a silver ground. His thick cuffs of metal inspired by African jewelry are particularly fine pieces.

Most of the jewelers of the day designed a wide range of acessories including compacts, cigarette cases, long cigarette holders that often matched bracelets and earrings, and dazzling encrusted handbags. The long lean lady simpering into her compact mirror or gesticulating with her cigarette holder is an archtypal image of the 1920s. Women flaunted their newly acquired freedom as much with their short dresses and short hair cuts as in the act of smoking or making up in public. Compacts, lipstick cases, vanity cases and cigarette cases were miniature *objets d'art* encrusted with jewels, hardstones, mother-of-pearl, shagreen or crushed eggshell, lacquer or enamel. Vanity

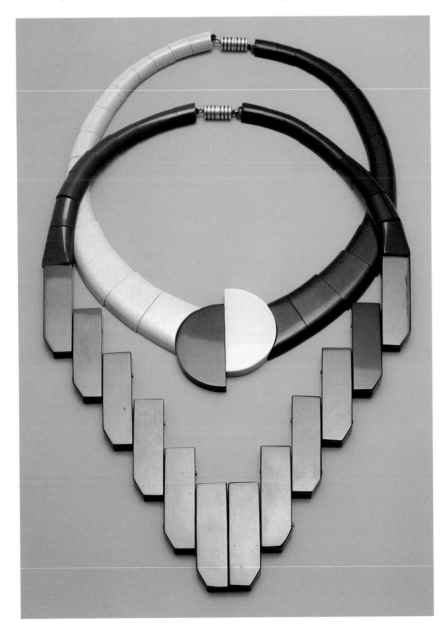

Right: René Lalique's molded glass pendant features the same fish-tailed sirens as his opalescent glass bowl (page 90).

cases depicting little Japanese, Chinese, Egyptian or Persian scenes were very popular. A *nécessaire* or vanity case contained compartments for lipstick, mirror, compact and comb, sometimes even a tiny watch face, and was often hung on a tasseled silk cord like a little handbag. A variation on this theme was the *minaudière*, devised by Alfred Van Cleef in 1930 and so named because of the way women presented themselves before its little mirror (*minauder*, in French, meaning to simper). The most precious of these vanity cases were encrusted with diamonds and precious stones. Cigarette cases were only marginally less decorative, often carved from jade, lapis or some other hardstone. Raymond Templier, Paul Brandt, Jean Dunand and Gérard Sandoz applied brightly colored geometrical motifs to their cigarette cases. Sandoz favored crushed eggshell, colored lacquers and silver. Handbags were lavish creations made of exotic fabrics, brocades and embroidered silks or animal skins, and the frames and clasps were studded with jewels. Sequined and beaded handbags were also popular. Decorative motifs were as fantastical as any that adorned the little vanity cases.

Georges Bastard designed intricate, precious, jewel-like objects and accessories; he was famous for his fans inlaid with patterns of contrasting shades of mother-of-pearl. He made jewelry in ivory, mother-of-pearl, jade and coral, and plain little boxes and bowls in materials such as ivory, rock crystal and agate.

Jeweled clocks were popular during the Deco period, and grew increasingly ingenious

in their design. The jewelers strayed over into the clockmakers' territory, while interior designers and *ensembliers* had also begun to produce their own clock designs. Of all the important jewelers, Cartier was most involved with clock design and produced some exquisite little jeweled clocks, known as mystery clocks because the mechanization was so cleverly concealed. The face was transparent, made of carved quartz, rock crystal or citrine, and the frame was usually built up of a quantity of other hardstones set with colored gems. Some were elaborate jeweled fantasies on the theme of Japanese or Egyptian temples.

Several designers of the period were drawn to the new synthetic materials available, and the possibilities they offered of creating bright attractive jewelry that was also cheap. Even as early as 1911 Paul Iribe was designing jewelry to go with the Poiret turbans; pieces that were cheap enough to be discarded when no longer in fashion. It was Coco Chanel, however, who made costume jewelry high fashion. Her designs made no pretence to be real jewelry and were intended to be worn with tweeds, sweaters and other informal day wear. Most of the large jewelry firms produced seasonal collections of costume jewelry in response to the fashion that Chanel had launched. The profusion of cheap manufactured jewelry exhibited at the 1925 Exposition showed how far this craze had caught on, with copper, silver,

Below: Bracelet cuff in silver, platinum, gold, onyx and diamonds, late 1920s, by Raymond Templier. The diamond and onyx brooch is detachable and can be worn separately.

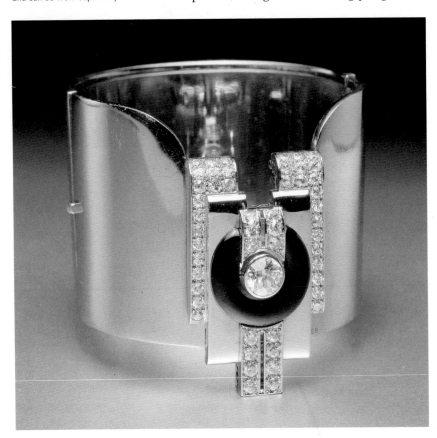

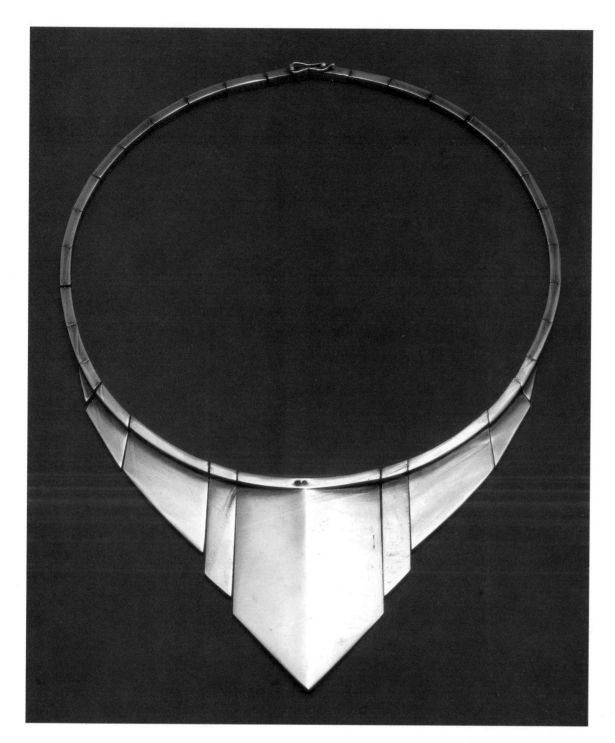

Left: Jean Desprès's silver necklace, c. 1925.

chrome, glass, fake pearls, enamel and some plastic being employed. From the mid-1920s bakelite and other synthetic resins came increasingly into use, first in mottled shades imitating marble, tortoiseshell, horn and amber, then in juxtapositions of bright colors. Other materials used were paste, base metal, and marcasite (little studs of cut steel). Cheap compacts and vanity cases were produced in vast quantities in chrome and enamel and decorated with bright jazzy designs in geometrical and zigzag patterns. It was French costume jewelry, more than anything else, that influenced jewelry design in other countries.

British jewelry of the 1920s was still dominated by the Arts and Crafts style, but by the 1930s cheap and cheerful designs had also become a feature of British production.

Fashionable ladies bought their jewelry where they bought their dresses and hats – in Paris, although many considered the bold Parisian designs to be too showy.

After the Wall Street crash of 1929, many jewelry firms were forced to close or to reduce staff to a minimum. Costume jewelry really came into its own then, and the stock Art Deco designs were reworked in plastic and brilliants. Multiple-use jewelry was one solution – brooches that became pendants, necklaces that became bracelets. Heavy bangles and African mask brooches carved in ebony and ivory became popular, and Mauboussin and Van Cleef and Arpels designed collections inspired by African carvings. Eventually the popularity of the Art Deco style began to fade; gold replaced platinum and angularity gave way to curves.

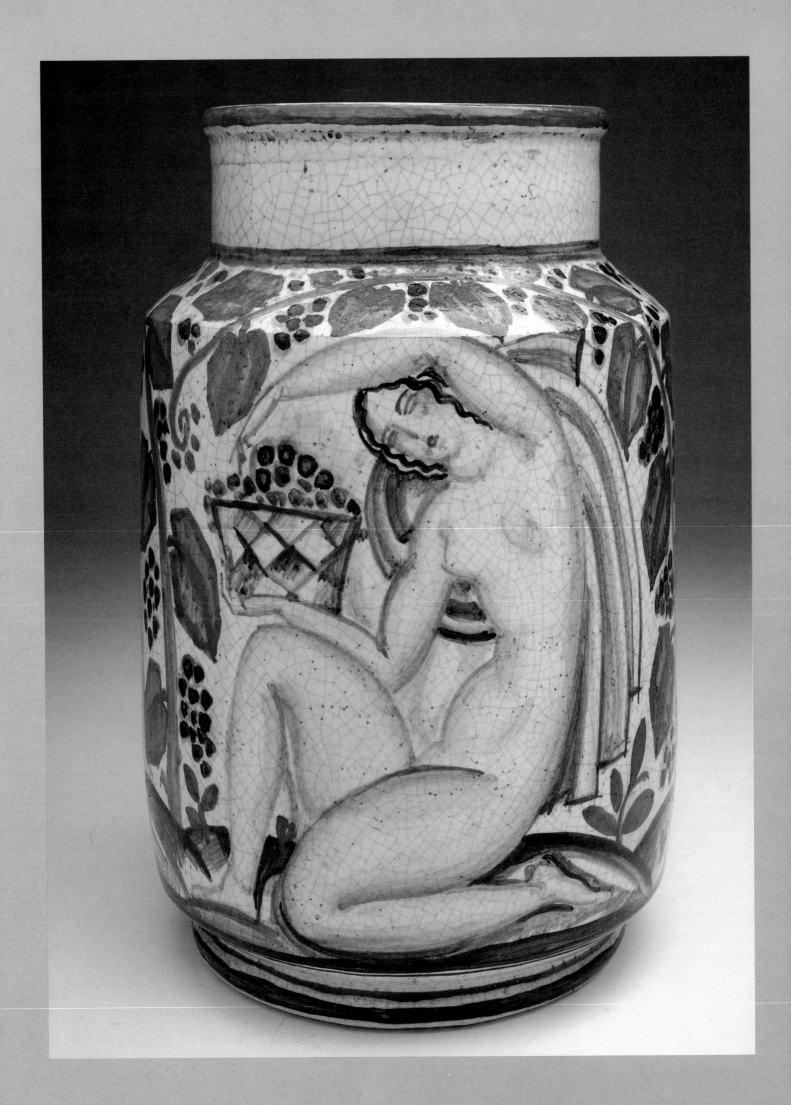

9
CERAMICS

Like the glassware of the period, Art Deco ceramics of good design and quality were produced in countries all over Europe. Styles were not necessarily dictated by the nucleus of French artists, although here as in other disciplines the French creative output was prodigious and influential. In fact styles were numerous and diverse, from the assertively hand-made creations of the studio potters through traditional manufacture to mass-produced tableware.

While manufacturers in the 1920s were beginning to turn out slick modern ware patterned with light Deco motifs, the studio potters, as if to assert the unique, hand-worked quality of their pieces, concentrated increasingly on craft traditions and obtaining a thorough knowledge of materials and processes of production. The period is marked by a return to the origins of the craft, and a renewed interest in the pottery of Persia and the Middle East, the Orient, Ancient Egypt and Rome.

A revival of interest in ceramics began in the late nineteenth century, and was stimulated by the prevailing fascination with Oriental art. A number of painters, sculptors and craftsmen became involved in designing ceramics and renewing links with the traditions of the craft. This interest in the arts of the East continued to influence the production of ceramics in the early part of the twentieth century. A complete mastery of technique, and particularly Oriental

techniques of glazing, became of critical importance to Art Deco ceramicists.

André Metthey played a key role in the development of a new aesthetic in the pottery of the period. He created a style that was based on traditional Middle Eastern designs, with an emphasis on rich colors such as turquoises, greens and pinks, a style that effected the transition between Art Nouveau and early Deco pottery. His study of Persian and Islamic pottery led him to switch from stoneware to faïence, with its greater potential for color effects. His designs were figurative and layed out frieze-like in bands or medallions. Most of his work predates World War I and many of the motifs that he introduced became standard to Art Deco. He also invited artists such as Derain, Matisse, Bonnard and Renoir to decorate his ware.

Another important pioneer was Auguste Delaherche, who worked in stoneware and porcelain and built up a considerable store of knowledge through his research and experiments, providing an excellent base for those who came after him. From as early as 1904 he began to incline towards simpler shapes and textured surfaces. He introduced the use of ceramic panels in architecture, which became popular in the 1920s.

Jean Mayodon worked in faïence and developed a style that was notable for its thick, crackled, polychrome glazes. Like Metthey he was most interested in color and spent his career experimenting to obtain a wider variety of rich colors. He frequently applied gold luster as a highlight, a technique gleaned from a study of Islamic ceramics. His decorative themes were drawn from classical mythology – stylized animals were particular favorites – and surfaces were crackled and textured to resemble antique pottery. Hand-painted and modeled figures and animals in faïence also feature in his work. In addition to small decorative objects he executed largescale ceramic panels and tiles, many of them commissioned for the great ocean liners.

From the 1910s through to the end of the 1920s, Emile Lenoble and Emile Decoeur reigned jointly in the field of ceramic design. Korean and Chinese Sung dynasty pottery were the primary influences on Emile Lenoble's hand-turned stoneware. By mixing his clay with kaolin he achieved a remarkably delicate and lightweight stoneware. His work is characterized by its simple floral, scroll and geometrical motifs, applied in bands to set off the beautiful shapes of his vessels. These were painted beneath the glaze, incised into the slip or else carved directly onto the vessel. His colors were rich and earthy; greens, reds and browns with creamy matt glazes.

Emile Decoeur's early career was spent experimenting with stoneware and porcelain

Below: André Metthey's pottery charger, c. 1920, reflects his Orientalizing style.

Opposite below: Jean Luce's white porcelain plates painted in silver and gold combine geometrical and semi-naturalistic motifs.

techniques, from drip-glazing to enameling or painted decoration. His early pieces are decorated in a floral style similar to Lenoble's work, applied in light relief to enhance the shapes. But his concern with harmonizing shape, color and the surface treatment of his wares led him to abandon conventional decoration altogether. His mature work dates from the early 1920s; forms are simple and elegant and clad in heavy, luscious, monochromatic glazes, while decoration is restricted to a little incised banding or a dark outline around the rim of a vessel.

The work of Lenoble and Decoeur shows clearly that the prevailing tendency was to simplify decorative effects and focus instead on texture, color and form. George Serré's thick stoneware vases, rough-textured and incised with chevrons and other geometrical patterns, are a good example of the move toward texture and simplicity of form.

Ceramicists of the period were fascinated with glaze techniques, and there was much experimentation with new glazes and revival of old ones. Edmond Lachenal was notable for having developed a kind of *flambé* glaze resembling cloisonné enamel, which he applied decoratively over a pale crackled ground.

The Fleming Henri Simmen was influenced by Oriental ceramics and traveled extensively in the Far East, studying the ancient traditions and techniques of the craft. As a result of his research he was able to devise a method of working using only organic ingredients and modeling by hand, rather than turning at the wheel. The shapes of his vessels were based on organic forms, and any chemical impurities in the material were manipulated for decorative effect. Occasionally he carved abstract motifs

in light relief to enhance his glazes, which were thick and crackled. Colors included a brilliant turquoise blue, often on a cracked ivory or beige ground. He made salt-glaze, with its attractive speckled effect, a speciality. His

Above: Incised and enameled sandstone vase, c. 1912, by Emile Lenoble.

Japanese wife, Mme O'Kin Simmen, carved delicate stoppers, lids and handles in ivory, horn and precious woods to decorate his pieces.

Earthenware was less popular in this period than stoneware and porcelain, but a few artists preferred its smooth glazed surface as a ground for their painterly decorations. René Buthaud was one of a number of talented artists from Bordeaux who worked in the Art Deco style. His fascination with African tribal art is reflected both in the forms and in the decorative themes of his work. His earthenware vases are large and bulbous, often resembling gourds and frequently painted with exotic black women against a background of tropical fronds and stylized animals. He worked in an expressive linear style, outlining his figures in black or brown and then frequently applying washes of color,

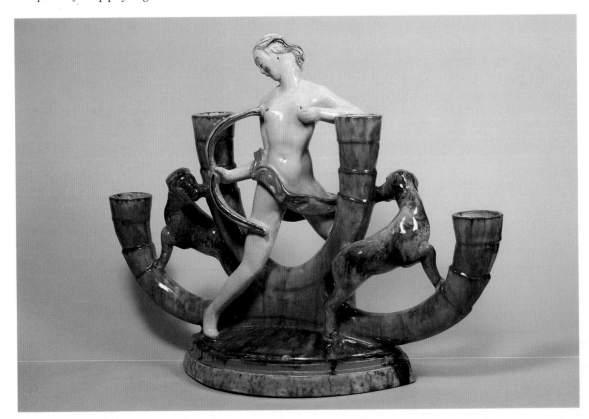

Right: Porcelain dancing figure, c. 1930, by the Parisian retailer Robj.

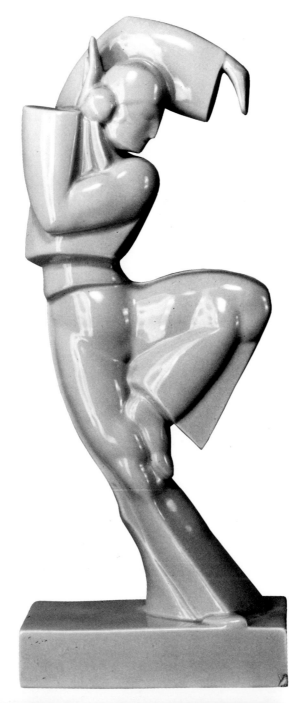

Below: Porcelain teapot decorated in the Russian Suprematist style, after a design by Chasnik.

usually over a crackled glaze. From 1913 until 1926 he held the post of artistic director of the Primavera ceramics factory. Francis Jourdain designed earthenware and varnished clay dinner services that were simple and robust-looking with minimal decoration, which he sold from his own shop.

In ceramics, as in other areas of design, the Wiener Werkstätte style lost some of its early severity. In the 1920s Susi Singer and Vally Wieselthier created roughly modeled pottery figures in lively drip-glazed colors, while Josef Hoffman and Michael Powolny designed simple and elegant modern tableware.

British studio pottery became important at this time, chiefly due to the talents of Bernard Leach, who studied in Japan and in 1920 set up a pottery in St Ives, Cornwall, with a young Japanese potter named Hamada Shoji. His work and teaching focused on folk traditions in pottery, and his special interest was in slip-ware. A number of his pupils became prominent potters in their own right, all working after his manner in earthy colors and undecorated slip. Katherine Pleydell-Bouverie, for example, developed a style of extreme simplicity and concentrated on perfecting a type of glaze made from wood ash.

Carter, Stabler and Adams were based in Poole, Dorset, and produced sophisticated handmade pottery for domestic and architectural use. This was decorated with floral designs in soft colors which display the influence of the Werkstätte potters.

Little porcelain figurines were popular during this period; a cheap alternative to chryselephantine and bronze statuary, they were often intended to be collected in series. They were generally highly stylized and included lively, colorful and often humorous caricatures of stars of the screen, stage and music halls, jazz singers and musicians. The Parisian retailers Robj sold figurines and decanters designed by a number of artists in addition to their other wares. The sculptors Joël and Jan Martel were well known for their series of animal sculptures in ceramic. Wiener Werkstätte artists Susi Singer and Vally Wieselthier worked in a figural style and splashed their appealing, roughly modeled pieces with vibrantly colored glazes. Clarice Cliff created original variations on the figurine theme. She designed two-dimensional cut-out shapes painted with lively dashes and spots of color to suggest the outlines of her figures. The Royal Dux company, originally of Bohemia (now part of Czechoslovakia) produced vividly glazed figurines in an exotic high Deco style.

The new creative fervor affected the ceramics industry as much as it did studio ceramics and, after a long decline in standards and endless degraded copies of past styles, the period saw the beginnings of a thorough moderniza-

Left: Porcelain tea service, late 1920s, by Edouard-Marcel Sandoz for Théodore Haviland.

tion of serial production tableware. The influence of the Bauhaus was enormous; though its specific contribution to ceramics was small, the strength of its ideals, and their successful application to other areas of design, helped to spread its influence, with most immediate effect on the ceramics industry within Germany. The Staatliche-Porzellan Fabrik in Berlin took on an ex-Bauhaus pupil, Marguerite Friedlander-Wildenhain, as designer. Her functional wares were virtually undecorated except for a little banding, while Trude Petri's 'Urbino' service of 1930 for the Arzberg Porcelain Works was absolutely plain.

An important influence on European ceramics was Soviet Constructivist porcelain, which was exhibited and much admired at the 1925 Exposition. Its dynamic modern style had much in common with Art Deco, but its propagandist and political content set it in quite another category.

In the nineteenth century a rift had occurred between the pottery industries and the individual potters and this separation still existed in the Deco period, particularly in France and Germany. The Arts and Crafts movement had done much to cause this rift, because the artist-potter, while gaining status, disdained industrial collaboration.

In the French ceramics industry the development of a modern style was slow and there were many misguided attempts to adapt to Art Deco. The Sèvres company, for example, made efforts to modernize its style but the results were often poor. One of its mistakes was to commission designs from well-known artists who had no experience of ceramic design,

though designs by Ruhlmann, Lalique, Dufy and the Martel brothers were more successful than most.

In general forms remained conventional or else, in a vain attempt to be modern, became aggressively angular. Decorative motifs more quickly reflected the prevailing fashions – although these were often insensitively applied. Theodore Haviland et Cie of Limoges

Below: Boldly geometrical tea service by Primavera, 1920s.

Opposite: This porcelain vase by Gio Ponti for Richard Ginori features a complicated three-dimensional effect of nudes and classical architecture.

Left: The classical simplicity of Jean Luce's teapot and sucrier, late 1920s, is relieved only by the scrolled handles.

was one of the companies which contributed a stylish and modernistic range of wares. Among the designers who worked for them were Edouard Sandoz, who created charming animal figures in porcelain, and Suzanne Lalique, daughter of the great *maître verrier*. Jean Luce designed stylish ceramic tableware and glassware, and was careful to modernize both form and decoration. The simplicity of his work reflects the prevailing tendency; his tableware, in particular, was cleverly co-ordi-

Left: Vegetable dish, 1930s, by Susie Cooper.

Below: This assortment of pottery pitchers and vases, c. 1930, by Clarice Cliff shows her use of juxtaposed bright colors.

Above: Stoneware and pottery vases, c. 1925, by Charles Catteau.

Below: The severe style of Keith Murray's vase for Wedgwood is in strong contrast to the work of Catteau.

nated with a scattering of geometrical motifs, either painted by hand or from stencils. Luxury services were decorated in gold or even platinum leaf.

The department stores offered a wide range of household ceramics, designed in their own studios. Of these the Primavera wares were the most successful. Süe et Mare produced their own tableware and decorative objects, which were invariably in off-white majolica and in the same floral style as their other objects.

After the Paris Exposition the style spread quickly through Europe, and many industrial potteries began to offer wares in a diluted style that was frequently insensitive, eccentric or even vulgar. A number of Belgian firms were more successful than French manufacturers in creating a Deco idiom suitable for mass-produced ceramics. The best Art Deco wares were produced by the Keramis factory, owned by Boch *frères*, whose most notable designer was the Frenchman Charles Catteau. Parisian high Deco motifs, especially the angularized rose, decorate his stoneware and glazed faïence in cloisonné patterns, often on a thick white craquelure or crazed ground.

The best Italian contribution to Art Deco ceramics was made by Gio Ponti, a versatile artist who worked in many disciplines. He designed ceramics for the factory of the Società Ceramica Richard-Ginori in an idiosyncratic style that was partly neoclassical in inspiration. His work acknowledged contemporary tendencies but was not dependent on them. Many of his ceramics are adorned with mannered female nudes reclining against architectural backgrounds.

Several factories in Denmark produced art pottery, in the contemporary style, including Bing and Grøndahl. They mastered a wide range of different techniques and had a number

Cubism had a pronounced effect on Czech decorative arts in the 1910s and this was apparent in some of the ceramic pieces produced, with their strange angular shapes and stark geometrical decorations, while more traditional potteries turned out designs equivalent to the Parisian high Deco.

Much of the Scandinavian ceramic output of this period displays a functionalist aesthetic, and in general artists were involved with industrial design. The work of the Swede Wilhelm Kåge is particularly notable. He was Artistic Director of the Gustavsberg Porcelain Works and designed tableware specifically for those with low incomes, as well as a series of stoneware pieces chased in silver with single stylized motifs on a greeny-glaze background – vases, bowls, plates and boxes – which he titled 'Argenta'. His simple faïence tableware drew on traditional design, but was at the same time functional and modern.

In the 1930s the professional industrial designer emerged to bridge the gap between art and industry, and was responsible for the design of simple unadorned mass-produced tableware, designs which were also adopted by plastics manufacturers.

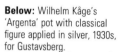

Left: 'Argenta' ceramic vase, 1930s, by Wilhelm Kåge for Gustavsberg.

of talented artists working for them, including Jean Gauguin, son of the painter, who sculpted in glazed faïence.

In Britain Susie Cooper and Clarice Cliff are the best known of those who designed Deco ceramics. Clarice Cliff brightened British tables with her highly original and colorful designs, the colors inspired by the Ballet Russes; strident combinations of bright purple and orange (the famous Art Deco orange known as 'tango') were her particular favorites. She began her career at the age of 16 as a transfer print designer for A J Wilkinson Ltd and in 1939 became artistic director of the company and the related Newport Pottery Company. Her wares, designed in series with names like 'Bizarre', 'Biarritz', and 'Fantasque', were relatively cheap and immensely popular. Her designs are bold and crudely painted; bright geometrical themes as well as fruit, flowers and fantasy landscapes decorate forms that are often somewhat angularized.

Susie Cooper, on the other hand, introduced a quieter note of Modernism into her designs. She was greatly influenced by French Deco and is said to have radically changed her style as a result of her visit to the 1925 Exposition. She spent her early career decorating blanks for Gray's pottery and set up her own company in 1929. Her work was elegant, and decorated with stylized patterns or simple bands of muted color. The New Zealand architect Keith Murray represented an even more starkly Modernist approach to design with his minimalist machine-age pieces made for Josiah Wedgwood and Sons. His classic forms were clad in monochromatic glazes in cool colors decorated only with a few engine-turned incisions or parallel grooves.

Below: Wilhelm Kåge's 'Argenta' pot with classical figure applied in silver, 1930s, for Gustavsberg.

VOGUE

Modes d'Automne, Chapeaux et Tissus Nouveaux

Revue Mensuelle

10
FASHION

Opposite: Georges Lepape's *Vogue* cover, Autumn 1927, is in
his characteristically mannered style.

A study of Art Deco would not be complete without mention of the revolutionary changes in women's fashion that took place in the first decades of the twentieth century. These changes reflect the profound alterations in the economic and social structure that were equally a factor in the evolution of the decorative arts.

In this period fashion and interior design developed almost in unison away from past styles, absorbing influences from literature, the theatre, ballet and the fine arts. Couturiers, designers and craftsmen all drew on the same sources of inspiration in their quest for modernity, and Oriental, Persian, and Egyptian art, even Cubism, were plundered for new styles and motifs.

Jacques Doucet and Paul Poiret, the great personalities of the fashion world, were instrumental in developing the Art Deco style and introducing new sources of design. Doucet was most important as a patron, imposing his taste to some degree on the artists whose work he commissioned, and helping to develop a strain of Art Deco that was less dependent on traditional sources and more in tune with developments in the fine arts. By setting himself up both as couturier and interior designer, Poiret imposed an even greater unity on dress and decor. To a lesser degree fashion designers such as Madeleine Vionnet, Jeanne Lanvin and Suzanne Talbot helped to endorse this alliance, by patronizing the most fashionable designers and by allowing their interiors to be publicized in the interior decorating magazines.

The Art Deco interior as setting or backdrop for fashion plates or photographs made frequent appearance in contemporary fashion albums. Poiret set the example by posing his creations among piles of plump cushions. Later fashion plates frequently depicted ladies gathering for cocktails in an immaculate modern interior fitted out with the latest Art Deco accessories. To advertise a new perfume, Suzanne Talbot had herself photographed reclining on her *pirogue* sofa against the lacquered walls that Eileen Gray had designed for her. Leitmotifs of the Deco interior such as the stylized rose, the exotic bird or the greyhound featured in the fashion plates, while Oriental or tropical scenes often served as backdrops.

The changes in women's fashions were bound up with the changing role of women in society. The importance of the revolution that took place can only be fully appreciated by returning to the beginning of the century and tracing developments from there. Nothing could have been more different from the overelaborate and constricting fashions of the turn of the century than the styles that were beginning to predominate 20 or so years later. In the early years of the century fashion was the exclusive domain of the wealthy – a display of utter extravagance. A lady of the upper classes was expected to make the business of dress her *raison d'être*, for fashion etiquette was highly elaborate and there were numerous changes of toilette to be made in a day. A mature, womanly figure was fashionable; women compressed themselves into tight-laced corsets

Right: Norma Talmadge in *The Woman Disputed* directed by Henry King, 1928. The floppy brimmed hat, dangling earrings, strings of beads and long feather boa were typical accessories of the 1920s. Note too the heavily outlined eyes and cupid-bow mouth.

Opposite: Coco Chanel in a jersey suit and sweater of her own design, and wearing the multiple strands of pearls that she made popular, 1929.

that reduced the waist to tiny proportions and arched the back so that the bust was thrown forward. All manner of cumbersome petticoats and undergarments were worn. Blouses and dresses frothed with lace and other trimmings. Hair was puffed and padded and crowned by gigantic, over-decorated hats which were secured with long pins. Women were strait-jacketed by their clothes which made it impossible for them to move freely and forced them into dependence on their servants and their menfolk. These restrictions reflected the more general social restrictions that women had to endure.

Since the 1880s women had been taking part increasingly in various sports, and here their elaborate clothes had become more and more of a handicap. A lady might risk her reputation if she were seen in bloomers riding a bicycle around the turn of the century. Even the female tennis stars were cautious of altering their costumes in ways which might be considered too radical, and until the 1920s they played in long skirts, stockings and hats. Around 1910 the bathing suit was introduced, which was less ridiculous than the Edwardian dresses worn with bloomers but was still long and voluminous.

The new dances, including the famous Tango and Charleston, that were imported from America necessitated greater freedom of movement; only the latest Poiret gown with side vents could cope with such frenzied activity. The new dances and the fashions that they gave rise to were endlessly inveighed against, but to little avail. Even before World War I nightclubs were springing up in most European towns, and the craze for these dances was to increase throughout the 1920s.

Poiret worked for a time at the Maison Doucet before taking a position at the House of Worth. There he was given the job of catering for the large numbers of society ladies who demanded that simple and practical dresses be made for them. This project proved too innovative for the Worth establishment and Poiret was asked to leave after only a short time, but he had learned a valuable lesson regarding women's attitude to dress. It is important to stress the role played by women themselves in effecting change, for they began increasingly to rebel against the expensive, time-consuming and unaccommodating fashions. Sensing that the way forward in fashion was to continue to simplify and straighten lines, Poiret set up on his own in 1904. His tailored costume, adapted from the motoring suit, was enthusiastically taken up; it was chic but, most important, it was comfortable and allowed greater ease of movement. Poiret claimed to have liberated women from the tight-laced corset by reintroducing the Empire-line dress. Although he did not banish

Above: Dresses by Paul Poiret from the *Gazette du Bon Ton*, 1914; the angular style of illustration complements the straight lines of the dresses.

Below: This illustration of a Poiret gown of 1911 by Georges Lepape shows Poiret's typical scatter of plump cushions.

the corset altogether, he certainly rid fashion of the distorting s-shaped corset and reverted to a line that followed more or less the natural contours of the body. Stomach and waist were eased out of their former constrictions and dresses hung straight from just beneath the bust. He devised a quantity of dresses in the Empire style, with ample sleeves and low necklines. He simplified styles, abolishing excessive ornamentation and concentrating on line, color and fabric.

By 1908 Poiret's style had begun to exercise a considerable influence on the development of fashion. His use of rich and exotic colors was partly stimulated by the extravagant, vibrant sets and costumes of the Ballets Russes. His early designs also correspond to the evolving Art Deco style in interiors, with its confusion of Oriental, folk and Persian influences, bright colors and patterns. Oriental costume was a great source of inspiration to him, and he adapted the kimono sleeve to his models, as well as introducing gowns that were wrapped, draped and tied with sashes, or coats that billowed out behind in the Japanese fashion. He dressed women in rich, woven silks and brocades, often in strident color combinations — in part a reaction against the delicate, pastel tones that were popular during the Edwardian era. He introduced exotic turbans and bandeaux embellished with jewels, plumes and aigrettes.

In keeping with styles of dress and interior so evocative of the East, as well as the sense of theater imparted by the Ballets Russes, make-up came increasingly into use and the fashionable face became bolder and more provocative, with heavily shaded eyes and perfect, cupid-bow mouth painted in deep red. Poiret's fashion plates of the 1910s depict graceful, stylized, dark-eyed females, tall and slender in the new straight styles.

Poiret was also responsible for the introduction of the color fashion album, in which his designs were illustrated by artists such as Georges Lepape, George Barbier and Paul Iribe. The concept was quite novel, and proved valuable publicity. Many of these plates incorporate little narratives, and depict modishly dressed women in early Art Deco interiors. The languishing pose introduced in these early plates became an enduring feature of Art Deco fashion illustration of the 1920s; decor and dress shared the same stylized gracefulness.

Just before the outbreak of World War I, further changes were made in women's dress styles. The long, tubular line was broken with a tunic that hung to the knees and in England, and to some extent in France, a long belted jumper of knitted material became popular. When war was declared in 1914, the initial assumption was that it would be a trifling affair of short duration, but it soon became clear it would be nothing of the sort. Women were needed to replace the men who had gone to the front, and they set to work in hospitals, factories, workshops and offices, adopting a style of clothing that afforded maximum comfort and practicality. Because of this need for practical clothing, as well as the need to conserve fabric for uniforms, women's clothes became very simple and standardized. Some women wore trousers at work for convenience, others simply raised the hems of their skirts, and a few even cropped their hair.

When the war was over the contribution of women to the war effort was recognized and earned them a new respect and greater independence. Among other things, they were reluctant to give up the more casual styles of dress they had adopted, and felt they had earned the right to introduce similar but more stylish innovations into fashion. Although fashion reverted to some extent to its pre-war phase, the sartorial freedom women had tasted could not be forgotten and styles now evolved faster in a search for the same degree of comfort and practicality. Nevertheless, no single dominant style emerged for some time.

It is significant that the leading couture houses that emerged after the war were run by women; Coco Chanel, Jeanne Lanvin and Madeleine Vionnet. The innovations they introduced were largely based on adaptations of men's clothing, and the ground broken temporarily during the war was now broken for good; hems came up, hair was regularly cropped, a few women began to wear trousers. The war had created a shortage of labor and more women than ever before were compelled to work, including rising numbers of middle-class women, war widows and those who had been impoverished by the war. They demanded simple, functional clothes with style and smartness, while the ever-increasing enthusiasm for sports and motoring generated more casual and liberating fashions. The young generation rebelled against convention, associating the carnage of the war with the stuffy and restricting society that had preceded it. A

1913 *Costumes Parisiens* 82

Robe pour dîner au Bois.

cult of youth developed, reflected in the fashion for the lithe, adolescent figure and a dynamic, sporting style of dress. Emphasis shifted from breast and hips to the limbs; shapeless, tubular shifts displayed to advantage long slim legs and arms.

Born of peasant stock, Coco Chanel had raised herself socially and professionally through determination and talent and was every bit a woman of the new age. From the start of her career as a designer she set about simplifying and paring down shapes, easing lines, creating a smart feminine fashion that

Above: Tunic tied with a sash worn over a draped skirt with dipped hem, illustration by George Barbier from the *Gazette du Bon Ton*, 1913.

Right: Sonia Delaunay's fashion drawings of 1922-23 show her preoccupation with simple shapes and bold geometrical patterns.

Opposite: Summer fashions in evening wear, Paris 1933, with the typical soft draping, slim cut and plunge back.

1922-1923

Sonia Delaunay

Below: Fashion of 1930 as worn by film star Norah Baring: silk chemise dress, neat cloche hat and fox stole.

was easy to wear, with elements borrowed from men's clothing and especially from casual, sporting styles. She loved tweeds and jersey fabrics and made muted earthy colors, and above all black, fashionable. She was instrumental in creating the sharper and neater 1920s style, designing jersey tunics, smart tailor-made suits, long waistless chemise dresses, long straight evening gowns which were often beaded, jersey wool dresses, and suits with simple cardigan jackets. Like the best designers working in the decorative arts, she exercised a rigorous discipline in her designs, simplifying and purifying forms, concentrating on cut and materials, controling ornament and using it to accentuate the strength of her design.

Sonia Delaunay designed fabrics for clothing as well as for decorating and upholstery, the majority of them patterned with bold geometrics in strong colors. While other couturiers took up the idea of reproducing the geometrical motifs of contemporary painting and design on cloth in a more tentative manner, Delaunay's fabrics seem fresh and dynamic even today. She sought to apply pattern in a way that would enhance the cut and rhythm of the garment when worn. Her designs for dresses were produced exclusively by the couturier Jacques Heim.

The flapper style, so often regarded as characteristic of the 1920s, did not develop overnight and was mostly confined to the period from 1925 to 1929. Skirts were not consistently short, nor dresses consistently waistless through the decade. In the early years hemlines went up and down, waists appeared and

MODELS · GERMAINE BAILLY

1912 Costumes Parisiens 42

Eventails de Paquin
D'après G. Barbier et Paul Iribe

established between the Parisian couturiers and Hollywood studios and stars. Fashion at all levels became big business, and the resulting enormous increase in publicity speeded up the evolution of fashion.

Much of the 1925 Exposition was devoted to fashion and in many ways the new styles reflected those emerging in interior design: simple and functional, barely ornamented or patterned geometrically, neatly shaped, and above all utterly modern and without precedent. And like the new furniture, the new styles of dress were also increasingly easy to mass produce.

This was a period when fashion was slowly becoming available to all women. As styles grew simpler, it became easier to copy models and make them at home, and large numbers of paper patterns were published in magazines. Chanel was one of the few couturiers who approved the fact that her designs were copied and made available to women of all classes. Now that dresses did not need to be fitted closely around hips and waist, ready-to-wear garments became available, mass-produced and machined. Because they were simpler and used less material, they were also cheaper to reproduce. The mass-produced clothes industry began really to take shape after the war. Fashion was gradually becoming a game all women could play, and those designers who

disappeared, skirts were alternately flared and straight. The bobbed hairstyle sported by Irene Castle and Isadora Duncan before the war began to become popular and in the late 1920s hair was cropped even closer to the head with the introduction of the shingle. By the mid-decade the new dress silhouette had taken over: very neat, sleek and tubular, and ending just below the knee. At the height of its chic the garçonne look consisted of cropped hair, close-fitting cloche hat to emphasize the small, neat head and a long, waistless, tubular dress. Many women felt compelled to flatten their curves with corsets that thickened the waist and sometimes reached right down to the knees. Coats with huge fur collars were worn and evening wear consisted of sleeveless shift dresses, either in silver lamé or else covered in beading and fringing, and close-fitting beaded caps. Floppy pyjamas were all the rage for lounging in. Materials were supple and light and patterns were often geometrical, reflecting the fashion in the decorative arts. Although Paris remained the chief generator of these new styles, the long slim look was better adapted to the American or English physique. Hollywood films arriving from America helped to promote and spread the boyish styles, and links were

Opposite: 'A practical dress for the country'; the 1920s chemise dress.

Left: George Barbier and Paul Iribe's fan designs for the House of Paquin, 1912, showing the influence of Diaghiler's Ballets Russes.

Below: *Art, Goût, Beauté* fashion plate, 1921.

Right: 'Fashion for a windy day' by George Barbier from the *Gazette du Bon Ton,* c. 1925.

Opposite: A 1930s evening dress showing the popular black decolleté.

Below: Bathing fashions of the 1920s showing the fashionable boylike silhouette.

did not recognize that fact and adapt to it were soon ousted; Poiret was among those who refused to give up the idea of a fashion for the élite.

In the last years of the 1920s hems began to descend again, due in part to a reaction against the folly and excess of the previous years, and also to the generally more sober atmosphere brought on by the Depression. Evening dress hems began to swoop to floor level, at first dipping at the back to form an absurd little train, while day dresses were worn just above the ankle. In other respects the new fashions were forward-looking and innovative. Like the style that predominated in the decorative arts, they focused on clever manipulation of materials and the use of new synthetic fabrics. This softer, more feminine style was a reaction to the angularity and masculinity of the 1920s. Hair

was longer but worn close to the head, and dress designs respected the natural contours of the body. Madeleine Vionnet introduced the bias cut which allowed the material to mold to the body, emphasizing neat waist and hips and flaring gently to the hem. She dispensed with fastening; these dresses simply pulled on and off. For those who were not shown off to advantage by these fluid creations, clever pleating, tucking and draping simulated the effect. Short, lightweight coats worn over dresses helped to emphasize the graceful lines and further disguise unsightly contours. Dresses were totally simple. Fine lightweight materials like satin and the new artificial silks were used, while the predominance of cheaper materials like cotton – even for evening wear – reflected the economic stresses of the Depression. Colors were soft: peach, salmon or eau de nil.

Sunbathing became immensely popular in the 1930s; bathing suits shrank to a minimum of decent coverage, and the backless dress became the rage. A fashionably tanned body could now be flaunted in a dress that dipped dramatically at the back. Long strings of beads, worn back to front, and embroidery and beading detailing enhanced the new cut.

As the Art Deco style began to wane, Elsa Schiaparelli came to the fore in fashion design. Fulfilling tendencies that had been apparent in other disciplines for some time, she introduced motifs derived from Cubism and Negro art into her designs. Then, from the mid-1930s she took fashion off in a new direction, developing a style inspired by Surrealism.

11
BOOKBINDING

Opposite: This binding by Paul Gruel has a lacquer medallion
designed by François-Louis Schmied and executed by Jean Dunand.

The craft of bookbinding was modernized by a number of talented French designers in the 1920s. Their efforts were part of a general rejuvenation of book production, which bred a new enthusiasm among book collectors. Bibliophiles amassed vast collections of elaborately bound volumes, which were often produced as rare *éditions de luxe;* printed on the most exquisite hand-made paper and copiously illustrated by the leading artists of the day.

From the 1880s, under the influence of the Art Nouveau movement, there was a renewed interest in all aspects of book production. William Morris was in part the inspiration for this revival, and helped to establish a new aesthetic concern with printing, binding, typography and illustration. In this period a number of bookbinders sought to create a new style based on a return to craftsmanlike techniques. They focused on intelligent manipulation of materials, and developed a decorative style that was based on the organic curvilinear style of Art Nouveau and owed nothing to historical pastiche. Marius-Michel was the leading binder of the day, setting an exemplary standard of technical accomplishment. In the Art Deco

period, binders inspired by the innovations of the late nineteenth century broke definitively with the traditions of floral ornamentation, and established a style in keeping with the modern age. It was usual then as now in France for books to be published with soft covers; those who could afford to do so had their volumes bound for protection by the binder of their choice. Bibliophiles recognized the importance of adding to the value of a publication with an exquisitely worked binding.

Pierre Legrain was the first of the Art Deco designers to explore the possibilities of modernizing the craft of bookbinding, but Jacques Doucet was ultimately responsible for its revitalization. Just before World War I Doucet had auctioned off his carefully assembled collections of antique furnishings and eighteenth-century books, in order to devote himself fully to the patronage of modern artists and authors. His subsequent collection of manuscripts and first editions by contemporary writers needed, he felt, to be bound in an appropriately original and contemporary style. André Mare was his first choice for the task, but was away fighting at the front. Legrain, recently discharged from the army on grounds of poor health and seeking employment, was commissioned instead. As it turned out, he proved a far more imaginative and innovative designer of bindings than Mare, whose pretty floral designs painted on vellum would hardly have launched a revival of the craft in the way that Legrain's did.

After some hesitant early experiments, with very little training and no previous experience but with continued encouragement from Doucet, Legrain began to develop an arresting modern style. His first essays date from 1917. His inexperience proved an advantage, allowing him to exercise his creativity freely without regard for the traditions and conventions of the craft. All the exotic and unusual materials being applied to furniture at the time he transposed to the new medium, although traditional bookbinders had never dreamt of such combinations. Indeed his designs required a remarkable technical mastery, and the most accomplished of the professional binders were employed to execute them. He inlaid shagreen, parchment, and snake and lizard skins of various tints on to a ground of brightly colored Moroccan leather and calf, which he tooled in gold, silver, platinum and palladium. Later on he used metal and wood as his basic materials and inserted little plaques of ivory, mother-of-pearl, enamel or lacquer.

Legrain's early designs are in a floral high Deco style, but he soon adopted a bolder, more geometrical idiom. He created abstract collages of different materials, some of them stamped for variety of texture. Characteristic of his mature style is the fine linear tooling that was

Below: This binding by Pierre Legrain, inlaid with colored leathers and tooled in gold, is an example of his mature, geometrical style.

Opposite above: Paul Bonet's set of half-morocco bindings for Proust's *A La Recherche du Temps Perdu*, edition of 1928.

Opposite below Pierre Legrain's binding inlaid with snakeskin and tooled in gold for *La Jeune Parque* by Paul Valéry, 1925.

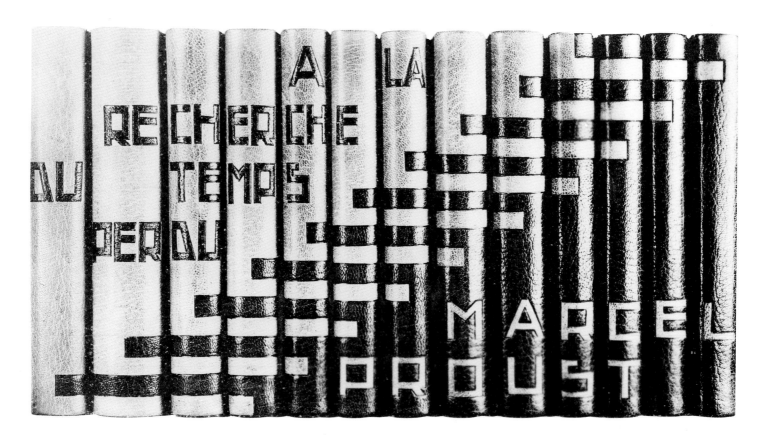

worked over the inlaid leathers. He was constantly experimenting with new materials, as well as with new designs and decorative devices alluding to the content of the book. Perhaps his greatest single innovation was his use of decorative lettering as the starting point for his designs. During his career, lasting little over a decade (he died in 1929), Legrain designed over 1200 bindings. His influence on modern binding has been enormous.

Of the older generation of binders who executed Legrain's designs, only René Kieffer was enthusiastic about the innovations Legrain was introducing into the craft. They continued to work together after Legrain left Doucet's employ and set up on his own in 1919. Kieffer himself made an important contribution to the development of a modern approach to bookbinding. He was trained as a binder and had set up independently in 1903, determined to devise a new style that owed nothing to the excesses of Art Nouveau. He developed a system of designing a single striking motif appropriate to the subject of a book, which could be repeated in different patterns and different colored leathers almost *ad infinitum*. By this method he created large numbers of original bindings at minimum cost.

In this climate of intense creative activity, with the example of Legrain's prodigious output to inspire them, there emerged in the 1920s a large number of talented designers specializing in bookbinding. They saw bookbinding as a chance to exercise and develop graphic skills, to experiment with new typefaces and incorporate lettering in a design. The challenge of inventing a simple, coherent design that evoked

the subject of the book was a considerable stimulus to ideas. One of a number of artists drawn from other disciplines to apply their

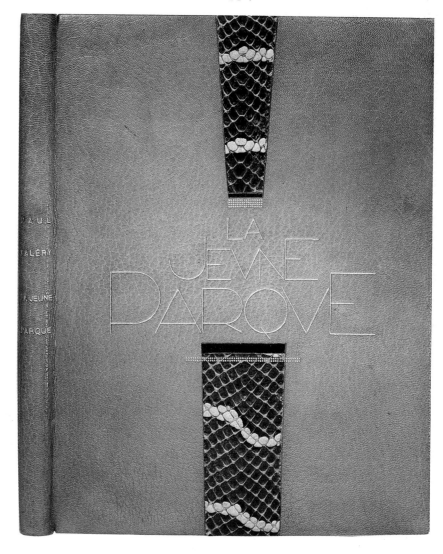

skills to bookbinding, the painter, illustrator and graphic artist Robert Bonfils first began to design and execute his own bindings around 1923. His work was mainly figurative, angularized in the Cubist manner and accented with gilt tooling. Graphic artists such as George Barbier, Georges Lepape and Maurice Denis also designed fine art bindings, as well as covers for cheaper mass-produced books.

The design of luxury bindings offered an opportunity to create unusual juxtapositions of materials and to indulge the current mania for surface decoration. The device of creating patterns in relief by raising sections of the wood or hardboard cover was popular with designers, but less so with the book collectors, who complained that these protruberances damaged other books on the shelf.

Lucien Creuzevault established himself as a binder in the first years of the twentieth century. After World War I he returned to his profession and began to concentrate on creating bindings for *éditions de luxe*. His striking collages were built up of different colored leathers, sometimes incorporating inlays of more unusual materials such as plastic or silver. An illusion of three-dimensionality or *trompe l'oeil* devices were characteristic features of his designs. Most Art Deco binders were influenced to some degree by the

dynamic style of contemporary graphic artists, and Creuzevault was particularly adept at creating simple but striking compositions in the manner of the best poster artists.

In the enthusiasm for decorating bindings, designs spread across the back, front and spine of books. François-Louis Schmied even extended his designs to the endpapers, which were of leather rather than the more usual paper or fabric. Most of his bindings were highly colorful and complex figurative designs, and many were inlaid with lacquer or enameled panels by Jean Dunand or Jean Goulden. He occasionally also worked in a more austere style.

Rose Adler, a follower of Legrain's and among the best of the younger generation of binders, was one of a number of women who chose to work in this field of design. As bookbinders women were not tyrannized by the antifeminine guilds and unions that dominated other areas of design. Adler was discovered by Doucet, who admired her work at a student exhibition and began immediately to commission bindings from her. She worked for him from 1923 until his death in 1929. Her early style was similar to Legrain's – like him she used combinations of materials juxtaposed in abstract patterns – but her designs were simpler, more severe and less busy than Legrain's, and her

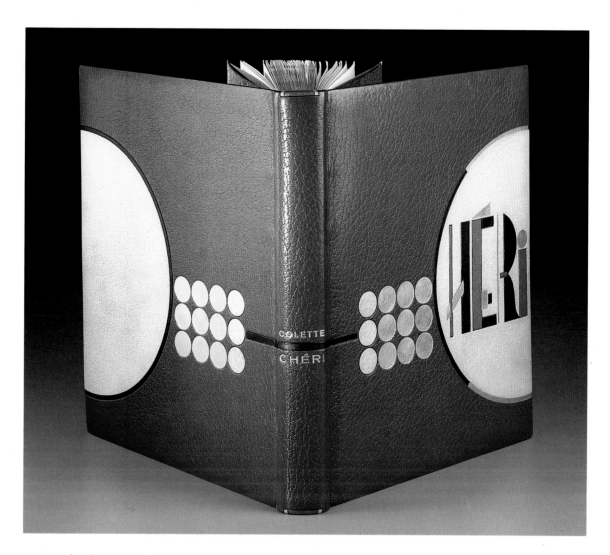

Left: *Chéri* by Colette, bound by Rose Adler and illustrated by Marcel Vertes, 1925.

Below: This binding inlaid with leather and palladium, 1929, by Paul Bonet shows his use of color and of bold geometrical shapes.

sense of color was always highly individual. Later on in her career she began to work in a figurative style, and to experiment with unusual materials: lizard skin, wood, cork, suede and precious stones. In 1930 she became a member of the Union des Artistes Modernes.

By the early 1920s book collectors were clamoring for modern bindings from Legrain, Adler and the other binders who were working in the Deco style. It became very fashionable to collect these *éditions de luxe*. Since the revival begun by the Art Nouveau bookbinders, the number of book collectors had been steadily rising. There were numerous exhibitions and bookclubs were started for new enthusiasts. Fashionable authors whose works were frequently published as *éditions de luxe* were André Gide, Anatole France, Paul Verlaine, Colette, Jean Cocteau, Oscar Wilde, Guillaume Apollinaire and Pierre Loüys. Each client demanded his own exclusive binding, and a designer might be required to devise any number of original covers for the same title. Legrain made a habit of donating to the customer the tools used for each binding, thus underlining the exclusive nature of his work.

The fine bindings and illustrated books exhibit at the 1925 Exposition was dominated by Legrain's work, and his influence was apparent in most of the bindings by other artists and craftsmen. In addition to the profusion of imaginative leather-based bindings, there were books covered in embroidered silks and other decorative fabrics, inlaid and painted, or bound with Japanese prints.

By around 1927 the great boom of *éditions de luxe* had begun to wane. The onset of the Depression only served to worsen the situation. Many publishers found themselves with unsold stock on their hands and some of them were forced to close down. Only a handful of the richest and most discriminating patrons continued to collect and commission *éditions de luxe*. Books had become over-wrought and vastly expensive, sometimes too precious even to be handled. When the fashion for intricate, complex and many-colored designs faded, binders sought out new and unusual materials. In the latter half of the period experiments were made using photographic images. Laure Albin Guillot was one of the first to explore this new area of design. She printed photographs on a variety of different materials and inlaid them in a leather binding or used them as endpapers. She specialized in microphotography, and used the abstract patterns made by enlarged plankton or other micro-organisms as unusual decorative bindings.

After Legrain's death in 1929, Paul Bonet came to be regarded as the most influential binder of his generation. He was of Belgian origin and trained as a fashion designer. His ad-

miration for Legrain's work made him determined to create bindings himself but in a new style, quite different from Legrain's. He began designing and executing his own covers from the mid-1920s. His style reflects the modernistic preoccupation with sculptural forms, play of textures and innovative use of materials, including semi-precious stones, ivory and above all metal. He developed a technique of cutting away a metal binding to display decorative endpapers beneath. From the mid-1930s, his experiments led him to transpose photographic images onto leather covers. His designs are simple and forceful, much less ornate than Legrain's. Bold zigzags, diagonals and geometrical forms decorate his work. His famous binding for the complete set of Marcel Proust's *A la Recherche du Temps Perdu* with the lettering and design spread across the spines of the 13 volumes, exemplifies the clarity, coherence and ingenuity of his designs.

The appeal of the *éditions de luxe* was by no means confined to their exquisite bindings. The finest handmade paper was used, and the best typographers and illustrators were employed to design them. François-Louis Schmied was a painter who became involved with the total design of a book – illustrating, printing on his own press, binding and sometimes publishing books himself. He took immense care in his work, sometimes spending up to three years on a publication, and it was

Below: Fernand Léger: illustration for *La Fin du Monde*, 1919.

C'est le

Dieu le père est à son bureau américain. Il signe hâtivement d'innombrables papiers. Il est en bras de chemise et a un abat-jour vert sur les yeux. Il se lève, allume un gros cigare, consulte sa montre, marche nerveusement dans son cabinet, va et vient en mâchonnant son cigare. Il se rassied à son bureau, repousse fiévreu-

not unusual for him to create a new typeface especially for one book. He sometimes collaborated with Rose Adler; he would illustrate and occasionally design lacquered panels, while she took charge of the binding.

Illustrators and painters often collaborated with top binders on an important edition. Paul Jouve illustrated books as well as designing ivory and bronze plaques for cover inlay. His famous series of illustrations for Rudyard Kipling's *The Jungle Book* were cut into woodblocks by Schmied and published by him in 1917. A 1925 edition of *Chéri* by Colette, bound by Rose Adler and with engravings by Marcel Vertès, is a good example of a collaborative production. Vertès was a Hungarian artist working in Paris, whose rather sketchy, sophisticated style was well suited to this particular text.

Illustrators tended to adopt the abbreviated, dynamic Cubist style prevalent in the fashion magazines, a style that was essentially linear, enlivened by generous washes of color. The languid, stylized young men and women of fashion illustration were equally a feature of these illustrated texts. Kees Van Dongen was popular as an illustrator in this genre, and George Barbier, Georges Lepape, Charles Martin and André Marty all contributed numerous book illustrations.

William Morris had revived the use of woodcuts to illustrate texts in the late nineteenth century. Because of their stylized quality and their stark contrasts, as well as their practical advantages over other methods of printing, they were immensely popular in the Deco period in both France and in England. The blocks were cut by the artists themselves, or by craftsmen who were often highly skilled in the art of rendering the image in wood. Raoul Dufy was the best illustrator of the period working in the Art Deco style. His first published and most important illustrations were his woodcuts for *Le Bestiaire ou Cortège d'Orphée* by Guillaume Apollinaire, published in 1911. Dufy and Apollinaire were friends and they collaborated on this volume, intending that it should be the first great illustrated French book of the twentieth century. In fact the book was not a success, despite the strong style of Dufy's woodcuts with their boldly contrasting blacks and whites. Many of his later illustrations reflect his fascination with the life of fashionable seaside resorts. Jean Lurçat, the famous tapestry designer, created some successful illustrations which were very similar in style to his tapestry designs. Other popular illustrators of the day were Marie Laurencin, Paul Véra, Jean Dupas, Dunoyer de Segonzac and Paul Iribe.

In England it was not until after World War II that designs for book covers really began to reflect the advances made by French designers. There were occasional attempts to emulate the French *éditions de luxe* and a few fine English

Above: Raoul Dufy woodcut illustration 'La Carpe', from *Le Bestiaire, ou Cortège d'Orphée* by Guillaume Apollinaire, 1911.

bindings were exhibited at the 1925 Exposition, including designs by Madeleine Kohn who worked as an amateur in Paris and London. As a rule book collectors who were interested in contemporary bindings used the Parisian designers.

French publishers were also far ahead of the English in the production of cheap but good-quality illustrated books. Many ideas borrowed from limited edition bindings found their way into mass-produced cover designs. In England the Nonesuch Press was among the very few publishers producing lively Art Deco cover designs. The British sculptor, typographer and engraver Eric Gill designed some highly stylized illustrations, often faintly erotic in tone, such as his woodcuts for Chaucer's *The Canterbury Tales*, which were executed in a style based on medieval manuscript illuminations. Edward McKnight Kauffer worked occasionally as an illustrator, as well as designing a number of book covers and dust jackets. Rex Whistler's meticulous, witty and vivacious style was well suited to book illustration. He was much in demand as an illustrator following the success of his illustrations for *Gulliver's Travels*, which were published in 1930.

There were few British illustrators working in a modern and innovative style, however, and book production in general lagged far behind that of the French. It was not until the 1930s that the delayed influence of French design began to take effect.

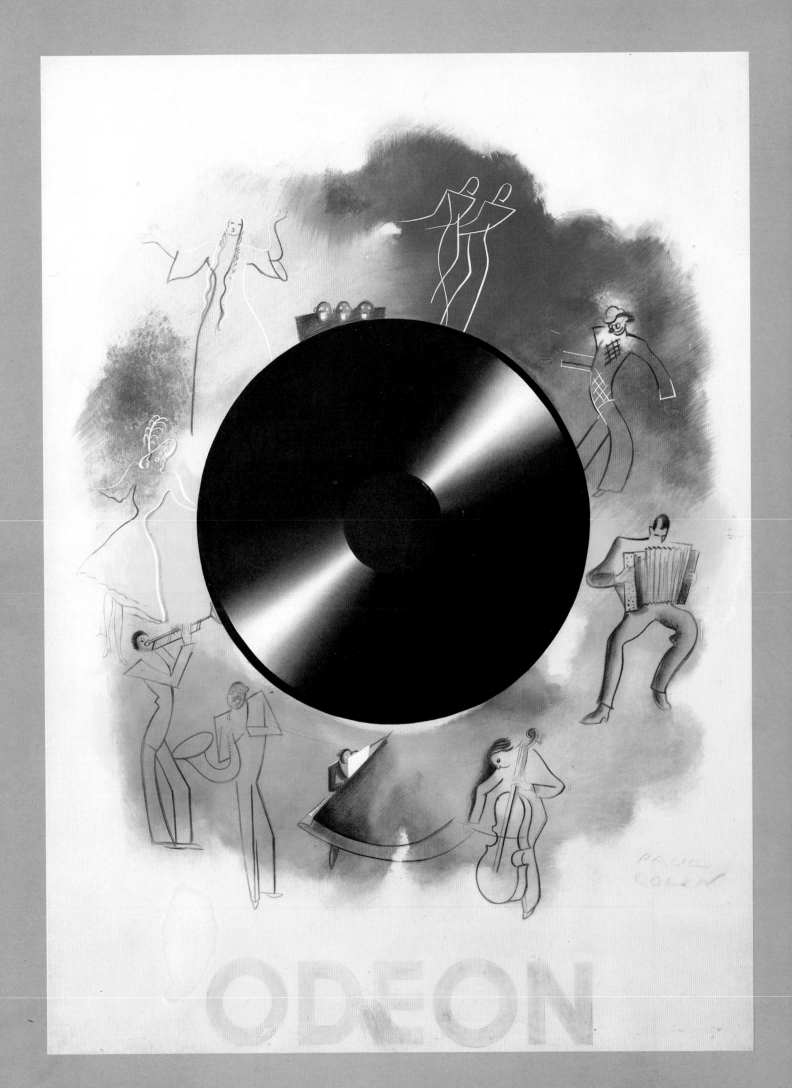

12 GRAPHICS

Opposite: Original maquette by Paul Colin for his *Odéon* poster.

Artists from almost every discipline were attracted to the medium of graphic art and contributed to the lively dynamic style of posters, magazines and commericial design during the Art Deco period. The commercial boom, which reached a climax in the 1920s, and the increasing competition among manufacturers that resulted from it, triggered an awareness of the importance of packaging and presentation of a product. Advertising up to this point had been in its infancy. Now the sophisticated psychological implications of associating a product with certain desirable qualities began to be explored, as well as the power of the image to convey that message and to act on the subconscious. Luxury, refinement, elegance and comfort were all sought-after attributes, while suggested associations with beauty, health and youth were also powerful selling points. Above all, in an age increasingly obsessed with its own modernity, the perceived attributes of modernity – primarily speed and power – were powerful evocations. Being essentially disposable art forms, the graphic arts encouraged experimentation,

and their proliferation and high quality during this period were remarkable.

The influences on Art Deco graphics were many; while fashion and magazine illustration reflected developments specific to the world of fashion and interior design, poster design and advertizing drew heavily on the influence of avant-garde arts. They sought to express the dynamism of the new age, which was best conveyed by the radical trends in the fine arts.

The beginnings of the new style in graphics can be traced back to the work of the Vienna Secessionists and the Glasgow school, with their linear typography and geometrical stylization based on a grid layout. Cubism, with its breaking down of forms, its angularity, its overlapping planes, was also an obvious influence on much of the graphic work of the period. At the same time the work of the Futurists, particularly their attempts to convey pictorially the dynamics of speed and the idea of power, was a rich source of inspiration to graphic artists. Many motifs of Futurist painting were successfully transposed to poster art. Likewise the work of the De Stijl group, with its pure colors and forms reduced to their essence, as well as Constructivist experiments in the fields of typography, photography and photomontage, exercised a significant influence on Art Deco graphics. In most cases graphic artists plundered these arts for motifs and design ideas. Only a handful of artists, such as Cassandre and Edward McKnight Kauffer, actually applied the principles of these art forms to their own designs.

The revolutionary teachings of the Bauhaus did much to develop a progressive approach to graphic design throughout Europe. László Moholy-Nagy, who taught at the Bauhaus from 1923, stimulated this new concern with graphic design, teaching the need for simple, rational compositions and for the reduction of the image to its most basic elements. He also taught a new attitude to typography, demonstrating the potential visual impact of type and showing how different effects could be achieved by varying the weight, size and arrangement of a letter. The Bauhaus artists Jan Tschichold and Herbert Bayer were innovative and influential typographers; Tschichold's *Die Neue Typographie*, published in 1928, was widely read by graphic artists. French artists in turn came to recognize the importance of lettering in graphic design. The simple and clean sans-serif type was first introduced in 1832 but was not used consistently until this period. In the 1920s and 1930s a number of new alphabets were devised, most of them variations on the sans-serif theme, which appealed strongly to the Deco artist. Some of these alphabets were streamlined and accented or geometricized, and are instantly recognizable as Art Deco in style.

Below: *Dubonnet* poster, 1935, by A M Cassandre shows his dramatic silhouetted design style.

pochoir process, a laborious method of printing that involved hand coloring with stencils, but which lent itself to brilliant color effects.

The Parisian magazine the *Gazette du Bon Ton* was the first to reflect the new fashions and the frivolous atmosphere of the 'jazz age', and drew into its orbit the new generation of young graphic artists; Charles Martin, André Marty, Umberto Brunelleschi, Erté, George Barbier and Georges Lepape were all regular contributors. It was launched by the publisher Lucien Vogel in 1912. Other magazines which gained immense popularity in the next years were *Vogue, Les Feuillets d'Art, Fémina* and *La Vie Parisienne*, with its slightly risqué Art Deco illustrations. In Germany the leading fashion magazine *Die Dame* was greatly influenced by Parisian trends.

By the mid-1920s the style of these illustrations had changed to reflect the angularity of the new fashions. Women were stylized to an even greater degree, with impossibly narrow bodies and long limbs. In the early 1930s photography began to take over as the domi-

Left: A M Cassandre's type specimen, typical of his radical approach to typography.

Below: Joost Schmidt's poster for the Bauhaus exhibition of 1923 features a combination of typography, geometrical forms and blocks of color.

In France fashion and magazine illustrations acquired a new aspect in this period, and were the first of the graphic arts to be modernized. Paul Poiret again played a decisive role in this branch of the decorative arts; it was his idea to publish albums of his latest dress designs as depicted by talented young artists, and his innovative fashions inspired the mannered elegance of the new style of illustration. Paul Iribe, in the fashion album *Les Choses de Paul Poiret Vues par Paul Iribe* of 1908, introduced an exaggerated stylization and elegance in his depictions of women that was quite unlike any previous fashion illustration. Under Poiret's influence fashion became steeped in the exotic arts of Russia, Persia and the Orient, as interpreted by the Ballets Russes designers. These in turn were absorbed into the work of the fashion illustrators. Artists such as George Barbier, Georges Lepape, Erté and the Italian Umberto Brunelleschi adopted a flamboyant, exotic and somewhat erotic Bakst-inspired style suitable to the fashions they were depicting. By the outbreak of World War I this style of illustration had become the dominant one in all the fashion magazines.

Other countries soon took their cue from Poiret and produced their own color albums. These albums, and subsequently many of the fashion magazines too, were printed by the

nant method of reproducing fashions, and by the end of the decade fashion illustration was all but extinct.

The obsession with decorating and reworking everything in the Deco style extended to the packaging of products, particularly luxury goods like fine stationery, cosmetics and cigarettes (which were almost a fashion accessory). Poiret and Lalique were both involved early on with designing packaging for cosmetics. Many companies used high-quality printing methods such as lithograph or *pochoir* prints. Strident colors and metallic foils were frequently used, and images evoking elegance and refinement patterned the wrappings. The presentation of a product became all-important as competitors fought for an edge in the market.

The presentation of the product through advertising became recognized as an important medium for drawing public attention. At that time the most potent form of advertising was the poster. The turn of the century had been a very fertile period for the poster, a period when

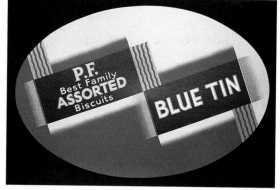

art adorned the streets and painters such as Mucha, Klimt, Bonnard, Vuillard and Toulouse-Lautrec contributed experimental designs. Toulouse-Lautrec was particularly innovative as a poster artist and introduced a striking, sometimes distorted perspective into his compositions as a means of focusing on his subject. World War I marked a break with the old style of poster art. The new style was generated by an increased awareness of the potential

Opposite: Paul Colin *Vichy* poster shows his use of simple images juxtaposed on a neutral background.

Left: This biscuit tin is decorated with geometrical Deco motifs.

Below left: 1920s Deco design for a Parisian eau de cologne; up-to-date graphics, bright colors and a touch of gold lend glamour to the product.

Below right: A M Cassandre's *L'Etoile du Nord*, poster for a luxury train, 1927.

of advertising, coupled with an impulse to celebrate the advancements of the machine age. Clear forms and contrasting colors replaced the sinuous lines of the Art Nouveau poster. At the same time new methods of printing meant that high-quality color designs could be produced in quantity. Posters were usually printed by lithography, which allowed a greater freedom of design and a wider typographical range. It also became possible in this period to print on a much larger scale than ever before.

Leonetto Cappiello was the first to break with the style of poster design established by the *fin de siécle* artists, and was regarded by many Art Deco posterists as responsible for the creation of the new style. He invented the strikingly effective device of associating a simplified image of an animal or human character with a product.

It was in the 1920s that poster art really came into its own. Artists quickly learned that simplification, stylization and abbreviation were crucial to the design of an arresting poster. They saw themselves as creating a means by

which the merchant or manufacturer communicated directly with the public. A message had to be at once striking and memorable, powerful and persuasive. Every device was exploited for its novelty and its ability to draw attention; dramatic perspectives, vivid color combinations, exaggerated stylizations and unusual lettering. A forceful, emphatic image was seen above all as one that was reduced to its essential components, the message broken down into symbols. Pure lines, pared-down forms and clear colors were favored.

Products and services particularly associated with the modern age, such as cigarettes, clothing, drinks, newspapers and travel, were advertized in a spare modernistic style. The enthusiasm for sport, physical fitness, fresh air and travel was reflected in poster design, while entertainment posters evoked the glamor and excitement of Parisian nightlife. The elongated highly stylized women who inhabited the fashion magazines were a popular emblem of modernity, but the images of trains, ships and cars, or even of steely machinery worked by a muscled arm, were more forceful evocations of the new age.

All the best posterists recognized the importance of integrating lettering into the overall design. Cassandre often used different typefaces within a single composition for variety and effect; he designed a number of new alphabets. Some artists juxtaposed handlettering and type, or invented a new typeface for a poster design.

Cassandre was the most brilliant of the poster artists of the period. He was born Adolphe Mouron of French parents in the

Ukraine, and studied at the Académie Julian in Paris. In his work he was known by his pseudonym, Cassandre, and often signed his work A M Cassandre. He first came to public notice with his poster for *Bûcheron*, which won a Grand Prix at the 1925 Exposition. In 1926 he established the Alliance Graphique advertising agency in partnership with Maurice Moyrand. His work best exemplifies the power, dynamism and clarity of Art Deco posters. By abbreviating images almost to the point of abstraction, he gave them a symbolic significance that made them lodge in people's minds. In keeping with this spare style he used few colors, sometimes only two, and never more than five or six. His travel posters are particularly stunning; perhaps his best known is the *Etoile du Nord*, an evocative design with its single pair of railway tracks vanishing into the distance beneath a lone star. After Moyrand's death in 1934 the firm foundered, but Cassandre's work continued to be as well known throughout the 1930s as it had been in the 1920s.

Four other outstanding French poster artists of the interwar period were Jean Carlu, Charles Loupot, Charles Gesmar and Paul Colin. Jean Carlu trained as an architect but turned to graphic art and began designing posters from the early 1920s. His youthful style was charming, a light rendering of Cubism, often based on overlapping geometrical forms and quite unlike the stark style of Cassandre. His *Mon Savon* poster of 1925 exemplifies his more mature modernistic style; the message is conveyed in a lively design that is reduced to near abstraction, dominated by red and blue forms. He designed a number of powerful posters in the cause of pacifism. Loupot was an illustrator and poster artist. Like Carlu, his early style was light and charming but became increasingly schematic, particularly after he joined Cassandre's Alliance Graphique agency in 1930. He was a brilliant colorist, often applying rough smudges of color to soften the rigid geometry of his designs. He made a striking poster for the 1925 Exposition that neatly summarizes the dual themes of the decorative and industrial arts; a rose is formed in the smoke emanating from two factory chimneys. The difference between this and the merely decorative poster that Robert Bonfils designed for the exhibition highlights the sophistication of Loupot's approach to design. In later years he adopted the airbrush technique; its smooth even quality of tone was well adapted to the modernist style.

Charles Gesmar's promising career was cut short by his death in 1928 at the age of 28. Up to that point he had designed for the great music-hall star Mistinguett, creating costumes and headdresses, sets and programme covers as well as posters. He worked in an attractive, fluid style that was obviously related to the

Left: Robert Bonfils's poster for the 1925 Paris Exposition.

Below: Paul Colin's *Revue Nègre* poster, 1925, helped to popularize the jazz age.

HORACE
TAYLOR

TO SUMMER
SALES BY
UNDERGROUND

BUY
BRITISH
GOODS

731 1000 26·5·26

VINCENT BROOKS DAY & SON LTD London W.C.2

Opposite: Horace Taylor's
Summer Sales, poster for the
London Underground, 1926.

Left: Otto Baumberger's poster
for the Swiss fashion house
PKZ, 1923.

poster art of the turn of the century. Paul Colin is best remembered for his entertainment posters, in particular those advertising Josephine Baker's performances. His first poster for the *Revue Nègre* of 1925 made him an immediate success. Other artists adopted personalities of the music hall and stage in a similar fashion to Colin and Gesmar. Kees Van Dongen designed posters for Arletty, and Charles Kiffer for Maurice Chevalier and Edith Piaf.

A number of artists from other disciplines contributed some striking poster designs during this period. René Buthaud is best known as a ceramicist but he also tried his hand at poster design, and these are decorated with the same plump nudes that adorn his stoneware vessels. Likewise the painter Jean Dupas transposed his version of the idealized female onto advertisements for the luxury trades. George Barbier and Georges Lepape, the

Right: Cover design for *The Studio* magazine, by Edward McKnight Kauffer, 1929.

fashion illustrators, also designed posters in their characteristically crisp and delicate style. From the world of ballet and the theater Natalia Goncharova, who designed for the Ballets Russes, created some bold, vibrantly colored posters.

In the 1930s, as the effects of the Wall Street crash made themselves felt, the competition among manufacturers and retailers intensified and the need to advertise became more acute. Constructivist and Bauhaus experiments with photography and techniques of photomontage began to influence the evolving art of the poster. Cassandre and Jean Carlu quickly adapted these techniques to their own designs, as did many other avant-garde posterists throughout Europe.

In most other countries of Europe there emerged a strong graphic style that had much in common with the work of the French artists. The Swiss-born Léo Marfurt worked principally in Belgium, but his poster designs were influential throughout Europe. His famous *Flying Scotsman* of 1928 was immensely popular, a design that bordered on abstraction yet con-

Below: A M Cassandre's poster advertising Triplex safety glass, 1931.

THE STUDIO
FOUNDED IN 1893

VOL. 97   NO. 434
MAY
1929
2/- net

THE
MIRROR   OF   ACHIEVEMENT

A.M.CASSANDRE

LE VERRE
TRIPLEX
S'ÉTOILE MAIS N'ÉCLATE PAS

veyed the speed and power of a train and the excitement of rail travel. Also working in Belgium at that time as an illustrator and poster artist, later to become a famous Surrealist painter, was René Magritte. His designs were archetypally Art Deco, brightly colored and featuring angular, fashionable young people.

In Switzerland the clothing store PKZ enjoyed an unrivaled reputation for exciting and avant-garde posters; Otto Baumberger and Herbert Matter were two notable posterists who worked for PKZ. Matter is famous for pioneering a technique of photomontage in the mid-1930s. The best representative of Austrian graphic design of the period is the Hungarian artist Marcel Vertès, who worked in Vienna for some time and whose light, appealing style had much in common with French design.

Germany evolved its own Modernist style early on. This was partly due to the innovations introduced by Lucien Bernhard. In 1903 his design for the match company Priester was very nearly rejected; it comprised simply two matches and the name of the product and was considered outrageously avant-garde. In the next decades a style emerged, inspired by Bernhard's work, that was more advanced than that of any other European country. Expressionism contributed an intense, forceful quality to German posters, which were generally more dramatic and highly charged than French work. Another pioneer figure of German graphic art in the years before World War I was Ludwig Hohlwein, who became a poster designer in 1906. His powerful, almost brutal style depended on dramatic *chiaroscuro* effects, vigorous line and a brilliant mastery of color. Hohlwein also developed techniques of printing for tonal effects, and achieved a quality of reproduction that resembled watercolor. He had a preference for depicting men rather than women, and in the 1930s his heroic, muscled types graced a number of Nazi propaganda posters. During this decade arresting posters in the Deco style became an important vehicle for Italian and German Fascist propaganda.

The British Beggarstaff brothers (really brothers-in-law James Pryde and William Nicholson), working at the turn of the century, were an important influence on graphic artists of the later period in Britain and elsewhere in Europe, although their designs had little impact at the time, being considered too avant-garde. Opposing the prevalent tendencies of Art Nouveau, they devised a style that was simple and bold, with subjects reduced to flat colored forms based on cut-out shapes.

In Britain too, competition among manufacturers and retailers intensified after the war, and advertising came to be recognized as a powerful means of manipulating public attention. As a result there was a corresponding increase in the number of artists specializing in this medium. The best early posters were devoted to advertising England's seaside resorts and the benefits of the various regional railway companies that conveyed people to these places, all competing for custom from Britain's holidaymakers in the days when foreign holidays were unheard-of for most people.

Much of the success of the style of graphics that evolved in Britain in the interwar period is due to the initiative and energies of Frank Pick, who became co-ordinator of advertising for London Underground in 1908. During a career that spanned nearly three decades, Pick was responsible for commissioning work from promising young artists and architects from both Britain and abroad. In 1916 he commissioned a sans-serif typeface from Edward Johnston which came to be known as Railway and was widely used in poster design. He also devised a highly successful poster campaign to promote greater use of the Underground. Edward McKnight Kauffer, Austin Cooper, Rex Whistler, Paul Nash and Frank Brangwyn, as well as André Marty, Jean Dupas, Man Ray and Laszlo Moholy-Nagy, all designed posters for London Underground under Pick's direction. Compositions reduced to flat colored shapes and forms delineated with sharp angularity became as frequent a feature of British poster design as they were of French.

Of the British poster artists, Edward McKnight Kauffer, who also made a number of avant-garde carpet designs and Alexander Alexeieff were the most brilliant. Alexeieff used watercolors for his railway posters to create a ghostly, insubstantial quality suggesting speed and the magic of modern travel.

McKnight Kauffer's poster art was emphatically anti-realist, and drew on Cubism and, particularly, the English avant-garde movement known as Vorticism. His work was not well received at first, being considered too radical, but eventually became very popular. He is best remembered for his designs for the London Underground and for the Shell oil company.

Soaring to Success !

DAILY HERALD

— the Early Bird.

13
PAINTING

Paris in the early decades of the twentieth century was a creative furnace, continuously generating new ideas and new theories of art. The mainstream of painters were constantly struggling to express some new notion of modernity, and formed various radical movements with the aim of expounding their theories. Other painters were less original and, while never wholly subscribing to the tenets of any one of these schools, drew on the superficial features of many of them to produce a style that was not Modernist, but rather a more conservative expression of modernity – harmonious rather than strident. It is possible to distinguish a 'sub-group' of essentially decorative works which can be identified with the Art Deco style, but distinctions easily blur and many works embody to differing degrees the combination of avant-garde and Art Deco elements. In many cases devices borrowed from these movements are mingled with motifs that are recognizably Deco.

It is significant that many of these painters worked also as decorative artists in a wide variety of capacities, contributing textile designs, graphics, fashion illustrations, designs for ceramics or lacquered furniture. As painters some became associated with certain interior decorators, working closely with them, exhibiting with them and creating works that would blend with their decorative schemes. Many paintings were executed to complement the interiors and furnishings of the period, some even with specific interiors in mind.

Throughout the Deco period paintings were rather sparsely hung; it was not until the 1940s that it again became fashionable to hang a quantity of pictures together. In high Deco interiors a painting played an essentially decorative role, helping to balance an overall scheme or to provide a focal point in a room. A sculpted relief panel or tapestry, a painted or lacquered screen or lacquered piece of furniture might be used for the same purpose. Paintings were often largescale, particularly in the monumental schemes of Ruhlmann and Süe et Mare (smaller paintings would in many cases have been hard put to compete with the richly patterned wallpapers). For public schemes and grand interiors, murals were fashionable.

Right: Nijinsky in *L'Après-midi d'un Faune,* 1913, by George Barbier.

Above; Erté's gouache *Les Fleuves; le Gange,* c. 1923.

Many of the interiors exhibited at the Salons and exhibitions were completely bare of paintings, indeed the addition of a painting would have upset their harmony. In Chareau's Maison de Verre, pictures were exhibited on easels rather than on the walls, an ingenious way of displaying them without disturbing the continuity of glass and book-lined walls. Other modernistic designers showed a tendency either to preserve the flow of the wall space – a designer like Jean-Michel Frank did not incorporate paintings into his *ensembles* but left the walls bare, covered only in some rich textural material – or to display a few paintings, carefully picked so as to enhance the balance of architectural forms.

Portraits and studies of fashionable women, nude and clothed, are an important category of Art Deco painting. That so many express a highly charged sensuality reflects the sexual liberation that was a characteristic of the times. Much of this work is slightly abstracted, in the Cubist manner, or stylized to convey elegance and refinement in imitation of contemporary fashion plates.

The work of Tamara de Lempicka best exemplifies this type of decorative portraiture. She was Polish, brought up in Warsaw, and when she was still in her teens she married the Russian Thadeus Lempitzki. At the end of World War I they came to Paris, escaping from the Russian Revolution. Finding herself in unaccustomed poverty in Paris, the resourceful Tamara took up painting to support herself and her child. At the Académie Ransom she studied under Maurice Denis and André Lhote. Of the two, the Cubist theoretician Lhote was

the more influential on her style. He taught her to break down a figure into broad areas of tone and color, and to 'disintegrate' a background. She became one of a group of moderates, consciously 'humanizing' Cubism. Her style owed something to the graphic style of the day, with its vivid colors, clean style and dramatic *chiaroscuro*. De Lempicka began painting professionally in the mid-1920s. Her subjects were fashionable and glamorous society figures, particularly women, and there was a strong element of eroticism in her work. New York skyscrapers serve as a background to many of her portraits. Her painting has a hard, brittle quality like enamel which contrasts with its highly sensual content, an ambiguity enhanced by the disdainful, arrogant attitudes of her subjects and which makes for a strange, rather disturbing element in her work. De Lempicka herself was a glamorous sophisticated figure, with a flair for self-publicity; she moved in the smartest circles and became much in demand as a portrait painter. Even her own setting was suitably chic; her apartment was designed by Robert Mallet-Stevens.

Jean Gabriel Domergue was another popular portrait painter, rendering chic Parisian ladies in an equally stylized fashion – long, elegant and refined in languid, fashion-plate poses. Another fashionable portraitist, Kees Van Dongen, came to France from Holland in 1897 and was greatly influenced for a time by the Fauves but later, in the 1920s, became a much sought after portrait painter of the Parisian *beau monde*. He portrayed nudes and society ladies in a highly stylized manner – wide-eyed and long-limbed. Jean Dunand executed some fine

also embodying many elements of the current decorative style. He undertook a number of decorative commissions, including frescoes for the Japanese Pavilion at the Cité Universitaire.

In addition to these stylized fantasies of society ladies, numerous paintings of anonymous women were produced during this period. The Polish-born Moïse Kisling settled in Paris after World War I and took as his subjects pretty, rather melancholy young girls, imbuing his paintings with a lanquid, sensuous air. René Buthaud was best known for his ceramic designs, but he also painted on canvas and created largescale works that were made up as stained glass or *verre eglomisé* panels. His paintings are in the same linear, colorful style as his ceramics, and generally depict the same stylized women.

The painter and printmaker Louis Icart worked in a style not unlike that of many fashion illustrators, bordering on sentimentality and kitsch. He was highly prolific and very popular, producing a quantity of paintings and prints depicting lissome ladies in fashion-plate attitudes, or streaming along with a pack of greyhounds in a blur of fur and chiffon. He helped to immortalize the chic *garçonne* of the 1920s; slender, active, provocative and invariably smoking.

Marie Laurencin was an important Art Deco painter, and one closely associated with the decorative artists. She was the sister-in-law of André Groult, who hung many of her paintings in his *ensembles* including his famous Chambre de Madame of the French Embassy at the 1925 Exposition. She also designed textiles

and highly textured, with broad areas of color contrasted with minutely detailed work. The Japanese Tsuguharu Foujita designed furniture, textiles and wallpapers, and was also a painter. His portraits of himself and his friends are executed in a delicate style deliberately evocative of traditional Japanese painting, but

Right: Painting in the *japonisant* manner, 1917, by Tsuguharu Foujita.

for him. Her early career was spent among many of the literary and artistic avant-garde, including Picasso, Apollinaire, Georges Braque and Fernand Léger. Contact with this group helped to form her style, although she remained independent of its innovations and its theorizing. Her work was highly personal and quite free from the constraints of tradition. She painted in soft, smudgy, pastel colors, and her subjects were kittenish women, does, doves, flowers and fruit – standard Deco motifs. Her paintings were very fashionable and, despite the pretty colors and subjects and the near-saccharine sweetness, in their way quite forceful.

With the new permissiveness of the 1920s erotic paintings became very fashionable, par-

ticularly works that dealt with lesbian themes. A certain erotic charge ran through almost every depiction of a female in this period, from fashion plates to portraits, but some work was more explicitly concerned with sex. The Danish painter, Gerda Wegener, became well known for her erotic paintings and risqué cartoons which were printed in magazines like *La Vie Parisienne*. She was one of a number of women painting erotic subjects that included the British artists Dorothy Wheeler and Dorothy Webster Hawksley. The work of the fashion illustrator and painter Alberto Fabius Lorenzi was more titillating than erotic; his women were elegant *fausses-naïves*, arranged in abandoned and lascivious poses.

The work of a group of artists from Bordeaux constitutes a category apart. Their paintings are generally based on a composition of female figures, often nude, and as well as being highly decorative in character have an unsettling, mysterious and erotic air. Jean Dupas is their most famous member; his paintings were admired by many of the leading *ensembliers* of

Left: Marie Laurencin's *Danseuses Espagnoles*, c. 1920.

Right: Gouache in ink drawing by Jean Dupas, 1928.

the day, and he frequently exhibited alongside their work at the decorative arts Salons. His paintings have been said to embody the spirit of the Art Deco style. The concern of the *ensembliers* for every detail of an interior extended even to the pictures on the walls, which were chosen or commissioned to harmonize with their decorative schemes and to create a focal point in a room. Dupas's work was commissioned to complement many Art Deco interiors of the 1920s and 1930s. Ruhlmann was perhaps his most illustrious patron, and chose to exhibit his large canvas *Les Perruches* in the Grand Salon of his Hôtel du Collectionneur at the 1925 Exposition, as well as commissioning a number of other works from him. Dupas himself stressed the decorative aspect of his work, stating that the various elements of his pictures were included to achieve a compositional balance, and that his pictures contained no meaningful content. Long, strangely angled, graceful females with stylized, expressionless features are depicted nude, or wearing tall hats and voluminous robes, alongside fashionable Art Deco animals such as doves and greyhounds. Every object is given a rather formalized treatment. In the early 1930s Dupas de-

Below: Jean Lambert-Rucki's *Negro Spirituals*, 1921.

signed a vast mural for the ocean liner *Normandie*, which was executed in *verre eglomisé* by Charles Champigneulle. The mural covered two walls of the grand salon and depicted the history of navigation. Fortunately many sections of it were salvaged from the fire which destroyed the ship in New York harbour in 1942.

Other members of the Bordeaux group were Robert Eugène Pougheon, Raphael Delorme and Jean Despujols. Pougheon studied in Bordeaux and Paris. He painted with a meticulous attention to detail and developed a method of stylizing which accentuated the fleshy, muscled quality of the men and women he depicted. Backgrounds were often strange and lonely landscapes, naturalistically rendered. Delorme painted mysterious nudes in a clean modernistic style reminiscent of neoclassical painting, often placing them against architectural backgrounds. Some of his paintings incorporate abstract Cubist motifs.

Animalier art was a popular genre in this period. Artists such as Paul Jouve, Jacques Nam and André Margat contributed a quantity of animal studies in a decorative modernistic style. Their work continued a tradition perhaps best exemplified in the nineteenth-century animal paintings of Delacroix and Géricault. The enthusiasm for animalier art was generated by a fascination with early art forms as well as things exotic; certain animals such as snakes and tropical birds were common motifs of the Art Deco vocabulary and appeared on furniture, ceramics, glassware and decorative lacquer panels. Elephants became especially popular after the great Colonial Exhibition in Paris of 1931. Most of the animalier artists adopted a Cubist approach to their art, with clean lines and a slightly angularized treatment of form. Animals were depicted leaping, poised to leap, or in attitudes that best suggested their dynamism and potential for speed. Generally they were not portrayed in their natural habitat but isolated against a plain background, a device which helped to emphasize the decorative play of contours and forms.

Below: *Amazone* by Robert Pougheon.

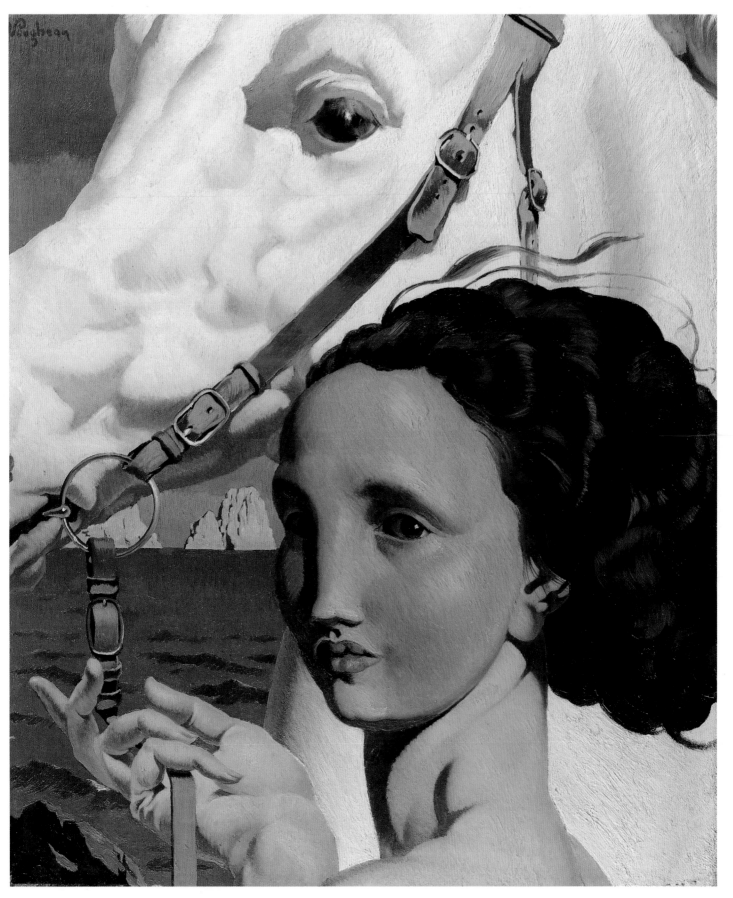

Right: Jean Dunand's *Josephine Baker* lacquered panel, 1927.

Artists took care to render the texture of fur, skin, feathers and scales. Jacques Nam concentrated mostly on cats, working occasionally in lacquer. Jouve was the best animalier painter of this period, and was highly prolific. He worked with Georges Cretté the bookbinder and with Jean Dunand, who transferred his designs to lacquer panels and plaques. His illustrations for Kipling's *The Jungle Book* – transferred to woodblocks by Schmied – were immensely popular.

Some artists fall into a category somewhere between Art Deco and the avant-garde movements. Gustav Miklos and Josef Csaky are two good examples. They were sculptors who also produced some gouaches and who worked in an idiom derived from Cubism and Constructivism, though their treatment of their subjects was essentially decorative. Similarly Roger de

Below: *Arnold Constable* poster by Jean Dupas.

ARNOLD CONSTABLE

COMMEMORATING THE MODE OF YESTERDAY

PRESENTING THE MODE OF TO-DAY

FORECASTING THE MODE OF TO-MORROW

Made in France. Tolmer. Paris

la Fresnaye exhibited with the Cubists but his work is more conservative in style. More famous as a sculptor, Jean Lambert-Rucki painted in a semi-abstracted style derived from Cubism and African art. Recurring subjects were black jazz musicians and African-style figures. Abstract art took some time to take hold among the Deco artists, and generally figurative compositions, mostly animals or fashionable young women, were preferred.

In Germany, Britain and Scandinavia many portrait painters adopted a style that can be classed as Art Deco. The Scottish artist John Duncan Fergusson was greatly influenced by French art, and developed a strong style that,

though formulaic, respected the individuality of his sitters. It is difficult to detect any of the frivolous spirit of Art Deco in German painting, which tended more to a forceful, intense style, sometimes charged with a perverse eroticism.

In England few painters were working in a decorative style akin to that of the French in the interwar period. Ernest Proctor is an exception. Mysterious, semi-mythological and highly stylized, his *Flora and the Flying Horse* of 1927 bears all the elements of a painting by one of the Bordeaux group. Frank Brangwyn was a master of the mural and received a number of commissions for municipal buildings. He liked to crowd his works with people – particularly muscular workmen – foliage and flowers. In the late 1920s he undertook a commission to paint 18 mural panels for the House of Lords. Ironically, although this was his finest work, the murals were deemed unsuitable and were never installed in the Palace of Westminster. Rex Whistler's painting, though not so obviously Art Deco in style, has a frivolous air in common with Art Deco and also a delicate, mannered, almost rococo quality that is derived from an admiration for eighteenth century styles. His murals for the Tate restaurant, executed 1927-28 and wittily entitled *In Pursuit of Rare Meats*, marked him as a young artist of considerable promise.

14
SCULPTURE

The nineteenth century witnessed a proliferation of decorative sculpture of all types, and particularly a fashion for large, ostentatious outdoor sculptures and public monuments. The sparer style of Art Deco gave less opportunity for so much sculpture but, like painting, sculpture was an important if not abundant element in the Art Deco interior, and continued to be applied as an architectural embellishment.

Rodin had come to dominate sculpture at the turn of the century, and his achievements cast a shadow over later work. Many sculptors subsequently sought to oppose his style of romantic naturalism and, like other artists seeking new inspiration, looked to primitive arts and the arts of Antiquity; to the flat and formal stylization of Egyptian and Assyrian art, and the crude abstractions of African-Negro art. Following the birth of the Cubist move-

Below: *The Island of Avalon,* stone carving by Jan and Joël Martel, c. 1930.

ment, sculptors sought to express in three-dimensional terms the innovations of Cubism.

Most of the sculptors classified here as Art Deco are identified as such by the essentially decorative nature of their work and, in the case of sculptors like Csaky and Miklos for example, by their tendency to interpret the innovations of the avant-garde in a more conservative and decorative manner. Many of the works discussed display an obvious relationship to other Art Deco pieces, particularly in terms of treatment and motifs.

Relief panels became immensely popular as architectural ornament in the high Deco period. Early precedents for this use of sculpture were the panels used by the Viennese Secession architects to decorate their relatively austere facades. These low-relief panels were a means of gratifying the mania for surface decoration that was particularly strong in the high Deco period. The panels were generally in a formalized classical style which combined angular contours and smooth surfaces. Female nudes, flowers, fruit and dancing figures were common themes. Shop facades, cinemas, theaters and some apartment blocks were embellished with these panels, as were grand entrance halls and dining rooms. The more austere modernistic Deco style emerging in the mid-1920s considerably reduced the use of these relief panels, however, while at the same time designs became highly angularized and abstract.

Free-standing sculptures were also popular in the high Deco interiors of designers like Clément Mère, Ruhlmann, Süe et Mare, Edgar Brandt and Paul Follot. These too generally represented female nudes, in a semi-classical style that often displayed a light Cubist treatment. Smaller-scale sculptures placed on desks, console tables or sideboards were also popular.

Of those working in the neoclassical style, Aristide Maillol and Antoine Bourdelle were the most gifted. Bourdelle's relief panels for Auguste Perret's Théâtre des Champs Elysées have often been cited as the first example of early Deco stylization. Other sculptors working in a similar idiom were Joseph Bernard, Alfred Janniot, Philippe Devriez, Marcel Bouraine and Richard Guino. Bouraine's work stands out as being smoother and more stylized than that of his contemporaries. Bernard and Janniot were chosen to create sculptural decorations for Ruhlmann's pavilion at the 1925 Exposition; Bernard made the relief panels that decorated the otherwise plain façade, Janniot the sculptural group that stood in the garden. This neoclassical revival culminated in the later 1930s in a heroic, fascist type of statuary, exemplified by the pieces made for the Palais de Chaillot, and the Museums of Modern Art for the 1937 Paris Exhibition.

By the start of World War I, a number of sculptors were beginning to absorb the innovations already made in painting into their own work, seeking to express Cubist theories in terms of three-dimensional forms. Jacques Lipchitz, Constantin Brancusi, Alexander Archipenko and Raymond Duchamp-Villon are some of the foremost avant-garde sculptors of this period. Their experiments were received with less enthusiam, however, than the works of the avant-garde painters. Their work was considered neither fine nor applied art, but fell into an ill-defined category somewhere between the two. Patronage was meager and many of the Modernist sculptors were forced to work in cheap materials such as terracotta, wood and plaster rather than in bronze.

Joseph Csaky, Gustav Miklos and the Martel twins belong to a group of sculptors who devised a less aggressive form of Modernism, absorbing influences from Art Deco as well as from the avant-garde. Their work eventually became popular as decorative objects in fashionable modernistic interiors.

The Hungarian sculptor Gustave Miklos had already begun to adopt a Modernist style before he left Budapest in 1909 and moved to Paris. He trained at the Royal School of Decorative Arts in Budapest and proved a versatile artist; in the years after World War I he worked for Jacques Doucet, designing carpets and objects in silver and enamel. In the early 1920s he made the decision to concentrate on sculpture, drawing on the influences of Cubism, Constructivism and primitive African art, and working mostly in bronze, wood and copper. His smooth, stylized, highly polished forms with their contrasting details of texture, occasionally enhanced with polychrome decoration, constitute a

Above: *L'Intransigeant* pavilion at the 1925 Exposition (Henri Favier, architect), with sculpture by Navarre and ironwork by Brandt. Large decorative relief panels were often applied to façades (as well as interiors) in the early Deco period.

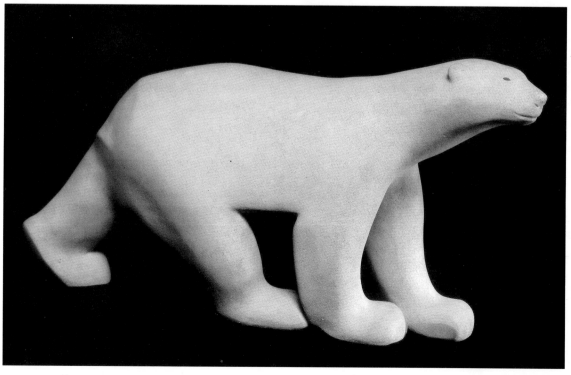

Left: François Pompon's *Polar Bear*, in white stone, c. 1922.

diluted version of avant-garde sculpture. Doucet continued to be an important patron of his work. In 1926, at Doucet's request, Miklos designed a decorative piece in rock crystal, silver and enamel to be placed on a small table by Rose Adler. The detailed specification for the commission underlines the distinctions that existed between much of the decorative sculpture of the Deco interior and the more innovative sculpture of the Cubists. In the Deco interior a sculpture provided a focal point but it was essentially a decorative object, a piece that played its part in the decorative scheme of a room. Miklos made other abstract sculptures from rock crystal, part roughly-hewn, part smoothly-faceted, sometimes illuminated from within. He also made a number of African-type masks, smooth, flat, elongated and highly stylized.

Like Miklos another Hungarian, Joseph Csaky, made the journey from Budapest to Paris, arriving in 1908. He exhibited with the Cubists and was much influenced by their work; his early post-war pieces are made up of geometrical forms in compositions that resemble the work of Fernand Léger. He was tireless in experimenting with new forms, as his work of the 1920s demonstrates, and evolved a very smooth, abbreviated figurative style.

Doucet set an important precedent by decorating his new Avenue du Bois apartment with African carvings and masks and avant-garde sculpture. In fashionable homes from the

mid-1920s the work of anonymous African craftsmen often mingled with pieces by Brancusi, Archipenko, Miklos, Csaky or Lambert-Rucki. Much of Lambert-Rucki's work was inspired by African art, and he created a number of masks and near-abstract sculptures that could be mistaken for authentic ethnic pieces. He was a Pole who had come to Paris around 1911 and shared a studio with Miklos for a time. He worked in an unusual style, though it was partly lack of funds that prompted him to mix materials like wood, stone, terracotta, glass mosaic tesserae and stucco, rather than cast in bronze. He collaborated with a number of Deco designers including Robert Mallet-Stevens and Jean Dunand. He and Dunand worked particularly well together and he created numerous designs for lacquer panels and furniture.

The twins Jan and Joël Martel were trained as monumental sculptors but, while they continued to make large outdoor pieces, they also executed many smaller sculptures. They were influenced by Cubism and worked in a strong style incorporating many harsh angles and zigzag motifs. They experimented with a variety of materials including concrete, glass, mirror, aluminum, zinc, steel and ceramic. Important commissions came from Robert Mallet-Stevens, who designed a house for them; they

Above: Sculpture outside the Palais de Chaillot in Paris.

Opposite: Joseph Csaky's *Adam et Eve*, a monumental bronze group, 1933.

Left: Jan and Joël Martel's *Le Joueur de Scie Musicale* (The Musical Saw Player), 1927.

Right: Granite figure of a condor, c. 1930, by Edouard-Marcel Sandoz.

Below: Marble sculpture of a monkey, c. 1930, by Edouard-Marcel Sandoz.

created lively, multi-faceted low reliefs depicting modern forms of transport for his Tourism pavilion at the 1925 Exposition, as well as the highly controversial concrete Cubist trees for the garden he designed for the exhibition. Their *Joueur de Scie* (Musical Saw Player) of 1927 was inspired by the musician Gaston Wiener. The sculpture is composed of sheets of zinc twisted to suggest the figure of the player bent over his instrument, a remarkably descriptive piece despite its degree of abstraction.

The animalier sculptors form a significant sub-section of Art Deco sculpture. Most worked in a stylized modernistic manner, sometimes exaggerating features, streamlining and smoothing surfaces or paring down forms almost to the point of abstraction. The Belgian Alberic Collin and the Italian Rembrandt Bugatti were responsible for leading the medium away from nineteenth-century naturalism toward a more expressionistic and abstract form of representation and a greater simplification of form. The great animalier painter Paul Jouve executed a small number of bas-relief plaques of animals, in a style that recalls Assyrian relief panels. His stylized treatment of his subjects also helped to influence the type of animal sculpture that emerged in the 1920s.

Greatest of all the animalier sculptors of the period, and most daring in his rejection of naturalistic methods of expression, was François Pompon, who first gained recognition when he was already in his late sixties. He had studied under Rodin and concentrated for much of his career on monumental outdoor pieces, at the same time experimenting with modeling animals. By the early 1920s he had developed the sleek, smooth-surfaced style he came to be known for, and his white marble *Polar Bear*, submitted to the Salon d'Automne of 1922, won him great acclaim. His method of stylizing was born of an attempt to express the subject not fixed in time, but as the sum of observed movements and attitudes over a long period. Surfaces were highly polished to catch and reflect light and to draw attention to the geometry of the forms.

Edouard Marcel Sandoz, also known for his humorous ceramic creatures which were manufactured by Haviland Limoges, made delightful animal sculptures of birds, fish and other creatures. He succeeded in conveying the character of each animal, despite the degree of stylization. In Austria Franz Barwig figured as a talented sculptor of animals. He evolved a dynamic style that combined realism with a degree of stylization.

British sculpture of the interwar period displayed some awareness of contemporary French movements and their influences. Many sculptors adopted a stylized classicism, others a Cubist angularization. Eric Gill combined both in his dynamic and powerful relief panels for the BBC building. Charles Sargeant Jagger was best known for his monumental outdoor work such as the Royal Artillery Memorial in London's Hyde Park, with its jagged Deco motifs and Assyrian influence. Elements of Egyptian, Greek and Assyrian art are evident in the work of Jacob Epstein, one of the founder members of the Vorticist movement and a sculptor whose massive, primitive and erotic works caused public uproar, although he did also make some quite conventional portraits. His tomb for Oscar Wilde of 1911-12 remained covered in the Père Lachaise cemetery in Paris for two years; its streamlined forms make it an important early manifestation of modernistic Deco. A number of artists made stylized portrait sculptures their speciality. Frank Dobson was a noted portraitist of the day, working in a style that smoothed forms and features, yet caught the individuality of the sitter.

Small statuettes of dancing girls, flappers, acrobats, athletes and children were produced in abundance in the 1920s and 1930s. Despite being commercial works and produced in large

Left: Maurice Guiraud-Rivière's *Enigma,* a white marble figure of a nymph, exhibited at the 1925 Paris Exposition.

Opposite: *Testris*, a bronze and ivory figure by Demêtre Chiparus, the most noted sculptor working in this medium.

Below: Demêtre Chiparus's cold-painted bronze and ivory figure of a cabaret dancer is typical of his exotic and detailed style.

Below right: *The Riding Crop*, patinated bronze and ivory, by the Austrian sculptor Bruno Zach.

numbers for the domestic market, they are often very appealing and immensely evocative of the tastes and fashions of the Art Deco period. They were designed to adorn a mantelpiece or side table, desk or dressing table; some were created as supports for lamp fixtures. Most of the statuettes were women, often scantily clad or dressed in exotic costume. They were idealized figures, lithe and slim and modeled in graceful attitudes, with the details of hair, features and dress quite realistically rendered.

These statuettes were made of bronze, a mixture of metals, ivory or a combination of bronze and ivory. They are referred to as chryselephantine pieces, though strictly speaking the term 'chryselephantine' refers to the combination of gold and ivory that was used to overlay some classical Greek statues. At the end of the nineteenth century the Belgian government began actively to promote the export of ivory from the Congo, making it available to artists and craftsmen at low cost, and organizing exhibitions of works in ivory. The French government followed suit, exporting ivory from its own colonies. In consequence there emerged a group of sculptors working almost exclusively in ivory, and 'chryselephantine' came to be applied to sculpture that incorporated ivory and some other material, generally bronze.

After World War I the technique of combining ivory and bronze was revived, and figures modeled on contemporary stars became immensely popular. The centers of chryselephantine production were Paris, Berlin and Vienna and the figures were sold throughout

Above: Edith Gabriel's *Mermaid*, 1926.

different textures – the soft, silky folds of a skirt, for example, contrasting with an intricately patterned top. Bases were carved in hardstones such as marble and onyx and were often quite elaborate. Chiparus's figures were produced in editions of varying sizes by several Paris-based foundries and manufacturers. The firm of Etling edited many of the high-quality figures that were produced in France.

The Hungarian-born Alexandre Kéléty also produced high quality chryselephantine statuettes. He worked mainly in bronze and specialized in complicated techniques, such as his method (known as damascening) of inlaying precious metals into a bronze ground to create an intricate decorative pattern. His figures are softer and plumper than others of the genre, their clothes more voluminous and their poses less athletic. Many of his works were given allegorical titles.

Another sculptor, the Belgian-born Claire Colinet, worked in a similar style to Chiparus although not with quite such fluency. Her figures were mainly exotic dancers, her subject matter inspired by the contemporary fascination with the arts of the Middle East and the Orient.

In Berlin, Ferdinand Preiss was the principal chryselephantine sculptor and his company, Preiss-Kassler, became the foremost producer

Europe, generally through jewelers and department stores. The best of these works are miniature masterpieces; despite being mass-produced they are intricately detailed and beautifully crafted. Achille Colas's invention of the pantograph made it possible to make accurate copies of an original, although the ivory carving and bronze work were always finished by hand. The bronze costumes were patinated or cold painted and sometimes gilded; some of the Parisian sculptors applied other metals to the bronze in the dinanderie technique.

Of the group of Parisian sculptors designing these figures, Demêtre Chiparus was the most important. His work was greatly influenced by the Ballets Russes and the prevailing enthusiasm for the exotic, Oriental style. He modeled statuettes of many stars of theater, ballet, music hall and cabaret in their elaborate costumes, from Nijinsky and other stars of the Ballets Russes to chorus-line girls. The ivory face and limbs were skilfully carved, but the real craftsmanship lay in the metalwork. His costumes are a remarkable record of the fashions of the day, all rendered in minute detail, the bronze elaborately patterned and chased to describe

Right: Alexandre Kéléty's cold-painted bronze figure of a young woman with a fan, c. 1926.

of these ornamental statuettes in Germany. He came from the town of Erbach, which had been a center of ivory carving since the mid-eighteenth century, and trained as an ivory carver himself. In 1906 he founded his company with Arthur Kassler, producing chryselephantine statuettes depicting classical figures. They were forced to close during World War I but re-opened in 1919 and adopted a more contemporary style, introducing a series of Olympic athletes and sporting figures, acrobats and dancing girls. The ivory was always exquisitely carved and the pantograph technique allowed the carvers to reproduce exactly the details of hair, features and gestures. Features were painted onto the ivory faces, and hair was tinted. The bronze costumes were chased and then cold painted, but not intricately patterned or finished to the high standard of Chiparus's work. Like the French figures, however, they were portrayed in striking and energetic poses. Preiss himself designed many of the figures, while other artists who provided designs were Otto Poertzel and Paul Philippe. Poertzel worked in a style almost identical to that of Preiss but Paul Philippe's work was rather different; his elongated, short-haired figures are more reminiscent of the women of the fashion plates.

Austria also had its sculptors and foundries producing these figures, and developed a recognizable style of design. The most important foundry at this time in Vienna belonged to the manufacturer Friedrich Goldscheider, and produced figures in bronze, ceramic and chryselephantine based on the designs of artists Josef Lorenzl and Bruno Zach. Much of Bruno Zach's work was quite overtly erotic. He modeled dancers and singers, girls in black leather or fancy underwear, whip-wielding or smoking with a defiant air.

The Austrian manufacturer Friedrich Goldscheider had established a branch in Paris at the end of the nineteenth century. Here in the Deco period decorative bronzes and terracotta figures were commissioned and manufactured and the foundry became quite important, independently of its parent company. At the 1925 Exposition the French Goldscheider foundry had its own pavilion and a remarkable list of contributors, including the Martel brothers, Pierre Le Faguays, Marcel Bouraine and Max Blondat. One of the company's most famous pieces is the *Faun and Nymph* group by Le Faguays. With its obvious debt to Cubism, its elements of Egyptian stylization, its semi-classical inspiration and its erotic overtones, it is a quintessentially Deco piece.

15
ARCHITECTURE

In the 1920s Art Deco architecture was mainly confined to France, with a fast-developing variant in America, but in the following decade the style became common in other European countries, where a number of quite distinct interpretations were developed. Art Deco architecture is generally eclectic and middle-of-the-road, incorporating elements of contemporary avant-garde styles and classicism, as well as Deco motifs from other decorative disciplines. In different buildings these elements are present in varying proportions; some lean towards a stripped classicism while others might almost be described as Modernist and few buildings are pure examples of the Deco style. In order to understand the nature of Art Deco architecture and the source of many of its features, an outline of developments in avant-garde architecture is required.

The radical movement known as Modernism that was to be the dominant influence on architecture after World War II originated in Germany before World War I. It was developed by the Bauhaus architects Walter Gropius and Ludwig Mies van der Rohe, and by the Swiss architect Le Corbusier among others. The new architecture was claimed to be purely functional and was often inspired by a utopian vision of a new, socialist society. It sought to express the developments of the machine age using new materials and applying new methods of construction and engineering. It

was conceived as a style completely in tune with the modern world, which owed nothing to past styles and which could serve as a universal architectural idiom. Modernism was greatly influenced by Cubism and De Stijl, particularly in its emphasis on the exploration of new conceptions of space. Modernist architecture was absolutely plain, stripped of all ornament, and often painted a uniform white inside and out. It was based on cubic forms, and composed of interlocking planes in the manner of De Stijl. Interior spaces were fluid and open-plan, separated by movable partitions and intended as multi-purpose living rooms. The sense of space and fluidity was further enhanced by large areas of glazing which flooded the interiors with light.

For all but a few in the vanguard of modern architecture, the Modernist pavilions at the 1925 Exposition were an important introduction to the new style. In the absence of a German exhibit, the Soviet and Czech pavilions and Le Corbusier's Pavillon de L'Esprit Nouveau represented the most radical expressions of Modernism amid the profusion of Deco ornament and debased classicism. Le Corbusier's stark white box of concrete, steel and glass with its main room rising through two storeys and filled with mass-produced office furniture provoked much derision. Ironically, although he aimed to display his contempt for Art Deco, his work was to exercise an important influence on

Right: Bruno Taut's Glass Pavilion was constructed for the Werkbund exhibition in Cologne, 1914.

Left: Willem Dudok's design for Hilversum town hall, 1928-30 is a variant of Modernism.

Art Deco architects, who developed from it a less rigid and austere form of Modernism. Even more aggressively avant-garde was the USSR pavilion designed by the Russian Constructivist Konstantin Melnikov. The framework was painted red and the facade was entirely glazed. A wide staircase leading up to the first floor cut through the pavilion diagonally and was 'roofed over' by a series of interlocking panels. The Czech pavilion built by Josef Gočár combined a Modernism inspired by German architecture with borrowings from traditional Czech architecture and an angularization derived from Cubism.

German Expressionist architecture, with its abstract, sculptural forms – free-flowing as well

Below: Robert Mallet-Stevens's design for the Bally shoe store in Paris combines simple forms with an element of decoration.

Right: Robert Mallet-Stevens's Villa Lipchitz, Paris, 1927.

Below: Auguste Perret's apartment block in the Rue Franklin, Paris, 1902-3, shows his debt to Charles Rennie Mackintosh.

as angular – and romantic obsession with glass architecture was a significant influence on Art Deco. The dramatic buildup of forms and decorative details characteristic of Hans Poelzig's buildings of the 1910s was particularly influential on Art Deco architecture, while Bruno Taut's dramatic steel and glass constructions provided a prototype for exhibition-building in the 1920s and 1930s. His Glass Pavilion built for the 1914 Cologne Werkbund exhibition, with its remarkable crystalline dome, inspired the design of the more prosaic Diamond Dealer's Pavilion at the 1925 Exposition built by Lambert, Sacke and Bailly.

In Holland, Willem Dudok practised a variant of Modernism, enlivened by a Cubist treatment of forms. Like the work of the Art Deco designers, buildings such as his Hilversum Town Hall represent a stylish adaptation of functionalism, with its assymetrical grouping of blocked forms, and dramatic contrast of horizontals and verticals; borrowing from the

stylistic features but not the underlying principles of Modernist architecture.

A stripped classicism dominated Scandinavian architecture of the early twentieth century and, though not itself classifiable as Deco, influenced a brand of English architecture that has much in common with Art Deco. Gunnar Asplund's early work exemplifies that tendency, although by 1930 he had evolved a style that owed more to the work of the international Modernists. In Italy too the Modern movement was slow to penetrate and a heavy classicism, embellished with modernistic or high Deco features such as stylized sculptural ornament, was the dominant mode up to the 1930s. The Italian pavilion at the 1925 Exposition and Milan Central Station of 1931 by Eugenio Montuori are good examples of this style.

In the early years of the Art Deco period there was very little being built in France that corresponded to the style in furnishing and interior design. In general decorative schemes were devised for rooms in already existing buildings, mostly dating from the eighteenth and nineteenth centuries. The 1920s were a lean period in France as far as building was concerned; after the ravages of World War I, work was concentrated on the renovation of existing structures rather than new building projects.

One of the most innovative architects of the early century was Auguste Perret, who began his career working in a transitional style that prefaced the Deco high style. He was much influenced by Charles Rennie Mackintosh and the Vienna Secessionist architects, as the rectilinear structure and decorative scheme of his apartment block in the Rue Franklin of 1902-3 suggests. But Perret's use of a reinforced concrete structure, which is allowed to dictate the forms of the building, gives it an airy and lightweight quality that is more akin to Modernist architecture. The flowered relief faïence tiles that decorate the facade are typical of the controled ornamental style of early Deco. The Rue Franklin apartments reflect the converging influence on Art Deco; Art Nouveau decorative flamboyance and the new forms dictated by Modernist technical advances.

High style Deco architecture was confined to Paris, where it was applied, often literally, to fashionable shopfronts and a few apartment buildings, in the sense that an ornamental Deco facade was simply grafted on to an old building style. Süe et Mare were responsible for the design of some of these shopfronts, which were generally dominated by decorative metal grilles cast into the familiar florid motifs of the high style.

It is a sad irony that early Art Deco architecture was best represented by the fantastic creations erected for the 1925 Exposition and pulled down six months later. The temporary nature of these showcases of Deco allowed for greater fantasy and freedom of design than was usual, and gave architects the opportunity to experiment with new forms, new materials and new decorative possibilities at whim. The results were often startling. The most flamboyant of these constructions were the four department store pavilions, which mingled ideas derived from contemporary styles such as Expressionism and Modernism with decorative motifs and forms of Egpytian, classical and Pre-Columbian architecture to create a highly decorative, lavish and dramatic effect. Features of these constructions that became typical of Art Deco architecture were the characteristic

Above: A Deco apartment block in Paris, on the Champs Elysées.

Left: Drawing by Robert Mallet-Stevens from *Une Cité Moderne*.

Right: House in Versailles by André Lurçat, who applied a decorative gloss to Modernism.

stepped pyramidal forms, and the use of expensive materials, decorative stained glass and relief panels. The stepped pyramid shape was in part influenced by the skyscrapers being erected in New York at this time, a design feature incorporated as a result of the 1916 zoning laws which decreed that beyond a certain height buildings should be set back in stages to allow light into the street. Pierre Patout's work represented a less extreme and more mature form of Art Deco, combining the proportions of classical architecture with a Cubist arrangement of forms and a functional sobriety. He built the Hôtel du Collectionneur to house Ruhlmann's exhibit at the Exposition, based on his design for Ruhlmann's own home; a dignified and relatively austere construction that was embellished with a little discreet sculptural relief in the stylized classical idiom characteristic of Art Deco. He was also responsible, with the architect André Ventre, for the design of the pavilions of the Sèvres ceramics factory.

Right: Pierre Chareau's Maison de Verre in Paris, 1928-31, inspired both Modernist and Art Deco architects.

The stripped classical Deco style was popular in France, as also in England. Perret's Théâtre des Champs Elysées of 1911-14, with its stylized sculpture by Antoine Bourdelle, and its stripped pilasters and cornices, represented a more sober classicism than his earlier work.

In France architects evolved a mature style of Art Deco that was more derivative of the International Modern style than of classicism. Architects took up the themes of space, light, plain white walls and cubic forms, and added their own expensive materials, decorative details and exaggerated features. In many ways this was a diluted and less austere version of Modernism. As an architect Pierre Chareau was strictly speaking a Modernist, though his interior and furniture designs fall more obviously into an Art Deco category. His greatest building was the Maison de Verre of 1928-31, built in collaboration with Bernard Bijvoët. Revolutionary in both conception and appearance, with its exposed metal structure and its facade entirely composed of concave glass blocks, this building represents a prime example of Modernist architecture in France.

The Maison de Verre was an inspiration to Art Deco architects. Robert Mallet-Stevens, like Chareau, was concerned with structural innovations and the paring down of forms. His buildings were conceived as abstract sculptures and the build-up of planes and forms displays a decorative capriciousness that would have been anathema to a Modernist architect. Nor are his buildings free from decoration; he often used strips of stained glass in abstract, geometrical arrangements to accent a feature of his design. He built shops, office blocks, factories, and a row of private houses in a street named after him. Other architects who reworked Modernism into a more decorative style were André Lurçat, Elise Djo-Bourgeois, Gabriel Guevrekian and Raymond Nicolas.

British architecture, as well as drawing on the themes and motifs of French Art Deco, was also considerably influenced by Scandinavian neoclassicism, and later also by Modernism, which was slow to arrive in England. Its introduction was due partly to the translation of Le Corbusier's *Vers une Architecture* which was published in England in 1927, and partly to the promotion of Bauhaus ideals by a handful of radicals such as the art historian Herbert Read. A number of young progressive architects were seduced by its doctrines, and in the Home Counties stark Modernist villas built for avant-garde patrons began to appear. These white cubes were the object of much derision, and indeed the flat sun roofs, vast living-rooms and walls of glass proved unsuitable to the climate. There were many more who adopted the stylistic features of Modernist architecture, without comprehending or committing themselves to the doctrines of Modernism.

In the 1920s this kind of debased Modernism was used for buildings that had no traditional precedent: garages, cinemas and swimming pools. In the 1930s the influence of modernistic French Deco helped to create a smart, commercial style suitable for luxury shops, hotels and restaurants, many of which were remodeled rather than rebuilt. Big London hotels such as the Savoy, the Dorchester and Claridges are good examples. To this was added a sleek streamlined style that was influenced by American Art Deco. The strange hybrid Art Deco that had been spawned in America in the 1920s in its turn influenced the developing modernistic style in France and particularly in England. Ribbon windows that wrapped around smoothly curved corners of buildings, the four-rung guard rail, and horizontal banding in contrasting color or material were all features of the American streamlined 'moderne' style that were taken up by English architects. The Peter Jones department store in Sloane Square, London, built by William Crabtree with Slater & Moberly and C H Reilly

Above: The wonderfully ornate New Victoria Theater, London, 1930, by E. Walmsley Lewis.

Oliver Hill, a prolific and versatile architect, was among the first to adapt the austerity of functionalism to a smarter, more sophisticated idiom. He was deeply interested by what he saw at the 1925 Exposition, and particularly admired the elegant and luxurious French Deco style. He developed a taste for sumptuous materials – glass, chromium, marble and alabaster, and a number of his buildings are also distinctly streamlined in style. Raymond McGrath's work displays the same sophisticated adaptation of Modernism. He designed the fashionable Fischer's Restaurant in New Bond Street, London, of 1932-33, which was fitted with a cocktail bar and restaurant linked by a wide curving staircase with polished steel balustrade.

Oliver Bernard's design for the remodeled foyer of the Strand Palace Hotel (1930) represents the gaudier aspect of English Art Deco. The foyer was dominated by an enormous illuminated glass balustrade and pillars. Bernard had worked as a theater designer, and was extremely popular in the early 1930s as a designer of spectacular and highly decorative restaurants and hotel interiors.

The talkies arrived in Britain in 1928 and there followed a frenzy of cinema-building. Most of these 'picture palaces' were built in the Deco style, often with streamlined modernistic exteriors and fantastical pseudo-Moorish, Egyptian, Aztec or Chinese interiors. Such dec-

Above: Interior perspective of Fischer's Restaurant, London, designed by Raymond McGrath.

(1936-39), shows the influence of American streamlined architecture. It is not surprising to learn that Crabtree had worked in New York for six months in 1928.

Right: The flamboyant interior of the *Daily Express* building, London, 1931-32, by Ellis, Clarke and Atkinson with Sir Owen Williams.

Below: Elevation of the river front of Hay's Wharf, 1930-32, by H S Goodhart-Rendel.

orative eclecticism was typical of French Art Deco furniture and interior design, and became as much a feature of the lavish Deco architectural style that developed in Britain and America. Cinemas were deliberately evocative of a rich lifestyle and were conceived as escapist fantasies, in a period when many were suffering financial hardship. The New Victoria Theater by E Walmsley-Lewis (1929-30) is one of the most spectacular of these Deco cinemas; its plain, modern facade is completely at variance with the fantastical decor within – an underwater world decorated with stalactites and scallop shells.

Many of the original Art Deco Odeon cinemas are still in use today. These were designed to a more or less standardized scheme, so that new cinemas could be built more quickly and at lower cost. Inside they were decorated with stylized murals, elaborate light fixtures and relief panels. Neon tube lights decorated their facades by night. The three principal designers for Odeon were Harry Weedon, Andrew Mather and George Coles.

The idea of mass-producing a style of architecture in order to establish a corporate identity was one that caught on rapidly in this period. Frank Pick, Chairman of the London Passenger Transport Board, was responsible for creating a recognizable house style for London Underground. He commissioned the now-familiar circular logo for the Underground from Edward Johnston, while Charles

Right: Osterley Underground station, London 1935, designed by Charles Holden in modernistic style.

Holden was assigned the task of building new stations for the lines that were being extended to the north and west. The stations were not identical, but they conformed to a certain type and were built in a modernistic style that was influenced by Scandinavian neoclassicism.

Industrial buildings were sometimes as indulgent, exuberant and decorative as those of the entertainment industry. There was no precedent for modern industrial building types in Britain, a fact which encouraged a degree of fantasy in some. The *Daily Express* building by Ellis, Clarke and Atkinson with Owen Williams (1931-32) is built in a typically Deco stepped pyramidal form, with curved corners and horizontal bands of clear glazing alternating with bands of black glass. The foyer is a flamboyant and showy display, decorated with sheets of highly polished metal and relief paneling, and a zigzag molding which conceals a lighting system intended to enhance the dramatic design.

The Hoover factory and the recently destroyed Firestone factory in London were marvelous examples of flamboyant fantasy Deco. The Hoover factory was built in 1932 and its architects were Wallis, Gilbert and Partners. Streamlined and white but without the lightness of structure of a Modernist building, its main entrance is decorated with brightly colored ceramic tiles in a scheme of chevrons, sunbursts and other geometrical details. Such neo-Egyptian decorative motifs were a popular embellishment for office and factory buildings, as well as cinemas.

Battersea Power Station, designed by Sir Giles Gilbert Scott, is a more dignified solution to the search for an industrial style. Gilbert Scott was originally a Gothic Revivalist but developed a variant of Modernism that combined an Arts and Crafts respect for high standards of workmanship. The power station is embellished with Deco details such as tiles, decorated bronze doors and stylized low-relief panels.

The head office for the Hay's Wharf Company by H S Goodhart-Rendel (1930-32) is an unusual building. Steel-framed and raised on stilts on its riverside front in order to facilitate the unloading of cargo, it is in some ways a highly functional and typically Modernist building. Yet its opulent Portland stone cladding, decorative relief panels and whimsical, faceted street entrance make it an important contribution to Art Deco design.

As in France, a stripped classicism was equally well adapted to the Deco style. Many of these buildings were influenced by the restrained neoclassicism of Scandinavian architecture. Charles Holden traveled with Frank Pick in Germany, Holland and Scandinavia, studying recent developments in architecture. He developed a style based on what he had seen of modern Scandinavian architecture, particularly the work of the Swedish architect Erik Gunnar Asplund, and adapted its comfortable modernity to his own designs; his Arnos Grove Station shows a specific debt to Asplund's Stockholm City Library.

Other important buildings in this style are

the London University Senate House Building (1933-37), also by Holden, Broadcasting House (1932) by Val Myers and the RIBA Building by Grey Wornum (1932-34). All are designed in a deliberately unprovocative mix of traditional and modern that is characteristic of Art Deco. The RIBA Building shows the influence of Asplund but also includes a wealth of Art Deco details. It is a lavish, finely crafted building, with rich, decorative plasterwork and sculpture, bronze doors and etched glass panels. Its over-scaled doorway recalls Assyrian or Egyptian architecture and is a typically Deco feature, used to provide a dramatic focal point on a facade.

In Germany there were isolated examples of building in the Art Deco style but the country's wretched post-war economy did not permit many such extravagances. The functional and cheap Bauhaus style provided a better solution to Germany's search for a modern style of architecture but here, as in Italy, the rise of Fascism put an end to much architectural experimentation, and Deco gave way to a monumental stripped classicism. The Bauhaus closed down in 1933, many of its designers and architects fleeing to England and America.

In retrospect we can see that Art Deco was a synthesis of elements from the contemporary avant-garde and classical styles, diluted and made palatable for an essentially bourgeois public; a style more in touch with public taste than with an elite avant-garde. It was also a style which met the needs of a contemporary lifestyle and had all the appearances of being modern without departing too radically from the traditional.

Left: Grey Wornum's RIBA building, London, 1932-34, has a simply-conceived façade with a wealth of Deco detailing.

It is not, however, a style that is easy to define. Its influences were manifold, and it could be flamboyant or dignified, sophisticated or vulgar. In architecture it was best suited to the design of fashionable villas and apartment blocks, and buildings devoted to recreational and leisure pursuits. But it could also be a dynamic industrial style, functional, modern and imposing, and well suited to the machine-age aspirations of the early twentieth century.

Left: Henri Sauvage's design for a Parisian apartment complex is a pyramidal fantasy which reflects both the geometrical purity of Art Deco and its soaring exuberance.

INDEX

ACKNOWLEDGMENTS

The publisher would like to thank Martin Bristow, the designer, Mandy Little, the picture researcher, Jessica Orebi Gann, the editor, Pat Coward, who prepared the index, and the individuals and agencies listed below for supplying the illustrations.

Architectural Association Slide Library/Photo FR Yerbury: 8, 27(bottom), 28, 73(bottom), 169(top), 181(bottom). **Victor Arwas:** 108(top), 110, 114(bottom), 119(top), 157(top), 165, 176(top),/Barry Humphries 163. **Bath Museums Service:** 129. **Bauhaus-Archiv:** 17(top), 55, 99(top), 145(bottom). **Bibliothèque Forney, Paris:** 54(left). **Bison Books:** 20. **Bridgeman Art Library/John Jesse:** 130/Victoria & Albert Museum 57(bottom), 126(top), 127, 131(top), 132(bottom). **Bröhan Museum:** 34(top), 44(bottom), 45, 95(top), 97(top), 116(top), 162(bottom). **Jean-Loup Charmet:** 14(bottom), 82, 122, 144, 149(top), 154, 158(bottom), 160, 183(top). **Christie's Colour Library:** 2, 14(top), 35(bottom), 57(top), 58, 59(bottom), 66(bottom), 67(top), 76, 77(both), 78(both top),

87(bottom), 91(both), 94, 95(bottom), 103(bottom), 105, 106(bottom right), 119(bottom), 134, 158(top), 164(both), 169(bottom), 172(bottom), 174(both), 175. **City Museum and Art Gallery, Stoke-on-Trent:** 119(middle). **Peter Clayton:** 15(bottom). **The Corning Museum of Glass:** 85(bottom), 86(top). **William Doyle Galleries:** 112(bottom). **Courtesy Alistair Duncan:** 30, 36, 38(right), 40(top), 43(bottom), 47(top), 67(top), 78(bottom), 88(top left), 103(top), 117(bottom), 120(top), 121(top), 137(bottom), 139(both),/Barry Friedman Ltd 162(top),/Christie's N.Y. 170, 172(top), 173, 176(bottom), 177(top). **E.T. Archive:** 15(top), 19(top), 32, 131(bottom). **Fondation Le Corbusier:** 29(bottom). **Barry Friedman Ltd:** 157. **Courtesy of Galerie Moderne Ltd:** 84, 86(bottom), 90(bottom). **Philippe Garner:** 33, 37(bottom), 40(bottom), 62, 69(top), 80(top), 81(top), 88(top right), 89(bottom), 116(bottom), 117(top). **Glasgow School of Art:** 10(bottom). **Greater London Photograph Library:** 81(bottom), 185. **Gustavsberg Fastigheter:** 121(bottom). **Lucien Hervé:** 43(top), 182(both), 184(bottom). **Angelo Hornak:** 6, 11(both), 18(bottom),

47(bottom), 50-51, 71(bottom), 87(top), 98, 102(right), 118, 171(top), 178, 186(bottom), 187(top). **Hulton-Deutsch Collection:** 125, 128(bottom), 133, 188. **John Jesse and Irene Laski:** 96(bottom), 97(bottom). **Herbert F Johnson Museum of Art/Cornell University:** 16(top). **The Kobal Collection:** 21(bottom),124. **J & L Lobmeyer:** 12. **London Transport Museum:** 150. **Lords Gallery:** 142, 146, 148(bottom). **Musée Bouilhet-Christofle:** 92, 96(top). **Musée des Arts Decoratifs, Paris, photo MAD/Sully Jaulmes:** 22, 29(top), 39(bottom), 42(bottom), 59(bottom), 70(top both), 71(top), 104(top), 113(both), 114(top three). **Musée de la Publicité:** 149(bottom). **Musée National d'Art Moderne, Paris,** 171(bottom). **Musée National de la Voiture et du Tourisme Compiègne, Photo Hutin:** 147(bottom right). **Museo di Doccia Sesto Fiorentino:** 115. **Museum of Modern Art, N.Y./Lillie P.Bliss Bequest:** 19(bottom). **The Robert Opie Collection:** 132(top), 147(top and bottom left), 152(top). **Collection Primavera Gallery, N.Y./Photo Courtesy Alistair Duncan:** 102(left), 104(bottom), 106(top and bottom left), 107, 109.**(c) Photo Réunion des Musées

Nationaux/Musée d'Orsay** 159/**Coll Walter Guillaume, Musee de l'Orangerie:** 160. **Rheinisches Bildarchiv:** 180. **Courtesy of The Royal Ontario Museum:** 13(bottom). **Royal Pavilion Art Gallery, Brighton:** 68. **Royal Institute of British Architects/Library:** 25(top), 26, /**Drawings Collection,** 183(bottom), 186(top), 187(bottom). **Van Cleef and Arpels:** 4, 100. **Victoria and Albert Museum:** 9(top), 17(bottom), 41(top), 42(top), 44(top), 48, 49(both), 52, 60, 61(both), 72, 73(top), 74, 80(bottom), 85(top), 88(bottom), 89(top), 90(top), 99(bottom), 120(bottom), 126(bottom), 128(top), 136, 137(top), 140, 141, 145(top), 153, 168, 181(top), 184(top), 189(bottom). **Vintage Magazine Company:** 18(top), 152(bottom). **Roger-Viollet:** 13(top), 24(bottom), 25(bottom), 27(top), 64, 65. **Virginia Museum of Art, Richmond/Sydney and Frances Lewis Art Nouveau Fund:** 10(top left), /**Gift of Sydney and Frances Lewis:** 10(top right), 34(bottom), 35(top), 37(top), 38(left), 39(top), 46, 54(right), 56, 66(right), 70(left), 79(top right and bottom), 108(bottom), 138, 166. **Stuart Windsor:** 189(top).